WOLVES
IN THE
KITCHEN

The Family Odyssey of Wolfpack Restaurant Group

by Scott & Nyla Wolf

with Emily Sutherland

To our kids, Ansley and Alec, for sticking with us through this crazy story. We are so proud of you. Also to your spouses, Tim and Maribeth, our grandkids, and future generations of our family.

Table of Contents

WELCOME TO THE WOLFPACK

Scott & Nyla

In the animal kingdom, a wolf pack is a fiercely loyal family. Whether that family has two members or thirty, each member has a unique role to fulfill. They fight the elements, navigate threats, and protect their own, not out of self-interest but for the well-being of their pack. It's a fitting metaphor to describe how a couple of "lone wolf" kids named Scott and Nyla found one another. Two kids who started with nothing and overcame the odds eventually built the Wolfpack Restaurant Group… with their kids. How? A lot of hard work with a few miracles thrown in.

People who know us have been telling us for years that we should write our story. Our response has always been the same. We would laugh.

"What story?" we kept asking. We're just Scott and Nyla doing what we do. Unlike a lot of stories you might read, our life is no rom-com movie plot. At times it has felt more like a battleground. We have fought *for* one another and *with* one another, sometimes at the same time. We still do. But, after forty years of marriage and thirty-five years of running businesses together, there is so much to be grateful for.

Through every tragedy, every sleepless night, every humbling conversation, and each tough decision, our life has been a series of unglamorous moments, losses, mistakes, and decisions that didn't come with any promises that we would be okay. We trusted our instincts, and we prayed a lot. We fought the odds because that was our only choice. We clung to our faith because, often, there was nothing else we could count on. We learned from our mistakes because the only other option was to repeat them.

When we reflect on the countless days when we were at our wit's end trying to figure out what to do next, we now see how helpful it would have been to know that someone else had made it through similar circumstances and setbacks. So, we write our story now, somewhat reluctantly, not because we have "arrived" by any stretch of the imagination. We are not experts in life, marriage, or business. If we are experts in anything, it's not giving up. But we want anyone who is reading these words to understand that if we can find the peace and stability that is now part of our everyday reality, so can you. If the two of us could create a legacy that can now live on for generations, anyone can.

Now, we have the joy of seeing thousands of people gather around tables across Central Indianapolis to feed their bodies and souls, share drinks with friends, celebrate milestones, and experience the power of community. In that process, we have personally grown and we've gathered around us an incredible community of staff members and family that make it all possible. The success and genuine joy we now enjoy once seemed like a distant speck on the horizon that we may or may not ever reach.

You never *really* know what is possible. We sure didn't. So, we hope our real-life experiences offer you a glimpse of hope. Because, no matter how bad things seem, whatever happens next could change everything. Come with us on the journey of building something pretty special out of almost nothing. Buckle up, because it's a wild ride! Don't say we didn't warn you.

Cheers,
Scott & Nyla Wolf

Still riding the waves after forty years together.

CHAPTER ONE

GROWN-UP KID

Scott

Tornado sirens began to blare in the middle of the school day. The teachers and administrators of Daniel Webster Elementary School led us students through the safety protocols every Indiana kid has to learn by the time we're in kindergarten. My classmates followed the protocols, lining up against the inside halls of the building, face down on their knees, heads tucked with their hands over the back of their heads. But I didn't line up.

All I could think about was Mom at home, alone, in a wheelchair. How would she ever get to the basement safely? She couldn't! I looked around me and saw everyone scurrying through the school hallway, distracted, while the sirens blared. I knew this was my chance to make a run for it. My dad was at work and my three older siblings were at school or out of the house by then. I had to be the one to save her.

So, I escaped out the side door of the school and ran toward home as fast as my legs could carry me. Rain poured down on me for the entire eight blocks between school and home. My heart felt like it might pound out of my chest when I finally reached the house, where my mom sat helpless. She had been diagnosed with multiple sclerosis just after I was born, and the disease had progressed over the years until she could no longer walk.

Mom was shocked to see me run through the front door.

"Scott, what are you doing?!"

"It's a tornado warning, Mom! We've got to get you into the basement!" I insisted.

I can't explain to you how a skinny nine-year-old kid who weighed less than 100 pounds managed to roll my mom, who weighed about 125 pounds, safely down the basement stairs in her wheelchair. I guess it was a combination of adrenaline and the hand of God. When the warnings passed, and I knew we were safe, I managed to get her back up the stairs, and then returned to school.

This story tells you all you need to know about young Scott Wolf. Even though I was the youngest kid in my family, my highest priority was always taking care of Mom. School, friends, and eventually sports all came after that responsibility. And though we didn't get hit by actual tornados that day, clouds were gathering over my world in ways that would forever impact me during the years that followed.

My dad began his battle with cancer when I was still a kid. He passed away when I was fifteen years old. By that time, I was the only one of my siblings still living at home.

Bernard "Bud" Wolf, 1909 - 1977

Mom's condition had steadily deteriorated during the previous few years. Since we didn't have much money and couldn't hire in-home care, a nurse came to our house to show me how to change mom's catheter, administer her medicine, and bathe her. I missed a lot of school, as well as football and wrestling practices, during that time. My football and wrestling coach knew a little about my situation and was supportive, allowing me to be captain of the team even though I wasn't able to make it to every practice.

Meanwhile, Mom and I had conversations no kid ever wants to have with his parent, and no mother wants to have with her son. We talked about what I would do when she was gone, and she recommended that I live with my sister. Looking back, I can't imagine how hard it must have been for Mom to have those conversations with her teenage son, but she knew she was going to die. And even though I had older siblings, they had their own lives. I didn't want my sister to feel responsible for me in addition to her own family, so I knew I would be on my own when she was gone.

I cared for Mom by myself at home until she got too sick for me to care for her alone. Then we moved in with my sister and her family until Mom passed away.

Laverne Wolf
1927 - 1979

I was almost sixteen years old when Mom died. At that point, I had to become an adult. My siblings sold her house to pay for all the outstanding medical bills and debt my parents left behind. They each ended up with a small sum of money and I got the van. That van was the only thing I had to my name.

A few weeks after we buried Mom, the high school guidance counselor called me in for a meeting. I'd missed a lot of school during the previous year or two, and she had worked with me to stay caught up. This time, when we sat down in her office, she mentioned that she noticed I hadn't missed a single day of school recently.

"Oh, that's because my mom died," I informed her.

Her face turned white, and she looked at me in disbelief. I hadn't talked a lot about what was going on, but at that moment I could sense her genuine concern for me. I was probably too busy surviving to fully process the loss of my mom or what a big deal that was for a kid my age. It was just how my life was unfolding and I didn't feel the need to talk about it.

My coach was one of the only people who knew she had passed away. He had a small two-unit rental property in town and allowed me to rent one of the units even though I was only sixteen and had no credit established. When I had moved in the few items I owned, I sat in that small apartment and wept. I was grateful for a place to live, but I felt so alone. I knew everything about my future was up to me. I needed to find a job immediately so I could pay the rent.

I found a job running a video store at the local mall, where I would work after school and practices. I didn't make much there, so before long I took on a second job. The owner of a local farmer's market hired me to unload produce trucks that arrived during the middle of the night. The middle of the night was one of the only times I was available for a second job, since days and evenings were filled with school, sports, and managing the video store. I didn't sleep much. I suppose the exhaustion, on top of the pain of losing both of my parents, wore on me more than I could identify at the time. I just knew I needed to finish high school, work to pay my rent, and stay disciplined in sports to improve my prospects of getting out of Logansport after high school.

One evening, after rushing home from practice, heating up dinner on the stove, and rushing back out to the mall for work, I got a call from my coach telling me the apartment was on fire. I couldn't believe what I was hearing. I was mortified. Immediately, I left work and sped back home as fast as possible to see what was going on.

When I arrived, I rushed in to see how bad the damage was and found my coach inside the smoke-filled apartment, which was no longer actively on fire. He held a garbage bag in his hands and was gathering dozens of beer cans from all over the apartment, putting them into the bag. When firemen first arrived, they had to kick in the door. It flung open and crashed into a huge stack of empty beer cans, which I'd hoped no one would find out about, sending them flying all over the place. Now, watching my favorite coach cleaning up my mess, I was doubly embarrassed.

I had found a little time to drink with my friends, needless to say. It was the '80s, and underage kids like us could stand outside the liquor store and pay people a few bucks to buy beer for us.

My coach never said a word about the beer cans. He was calm and said the damage wasn't too bad, mostly a lot of smoke from the burned food. He told me he would get the lock on the door fixed right away and never once reprimanded me for my mistake. I was hard enough on myself about it, and I'm sure he knew that.

I learned a lot about managing and leading people from that coach. He had my back and put in a good word for me whenever possible. Thanks to him I was bound for Ball State University in my home state after graduation. I finally got out of Logansport, and for the first time in years, I felt hopeful about the future.

Still winning matches for Logansport High School
while raising myself.

CHAPTER TWO

A DIFFERENT REALITY

Nyla

Unlike Scott, I came from a family with money, a big house, nice cars, and a membership to the country club. My parents were church-going people. Appearances and performance were important. Too important, in my opinion, because I didn't care about

impressing people or trying to be perfect. I was the
only one out of their four daughters who always
said whatever I thought, which I know felt
annoying and disruptive to the rest of the family.

My mom was always a stay-at-home mom
with a quiet, somewhat reserved personality. She
did all the cleaning and cooking, and did
everyone's laundry in the house. The way she
expressed her love for our family was by taking
care of everything at home for us. She liked things
done a certain way and preferred for us to let her
do them her way. I never learned to cook or clean
when I was growing up because I never had to. I
wanted to be out doing things and having fun
anyway. I didn't want to be stuck at home doing
housekeeping chores, and she seemed to enjoy
doing that.

My dad was the parent who pushed us to
achieve, get jobs, work hard, and earn a good
living. He had a big, talkative personality, made
friends easily, and knew how to get things done.

My grandma, Dad's mother, was the one person in the family who seemed to understand me. She always made me feel known and cared for. She always had plenty of time for me, so we spent countless hours together. Grandma lived next door to us until I was twelve years old, and my aunt lived next to her, which I loved. I loved knowing they were always nearby.

Grandma taught me about unconditional love by modeling it in her own life. She accepted me just as I was and showed me how to make memories. She threw parties, planned outings and trips, and celebrated special occasions in a way that I would never forget.

Grandma Peelen (far left)
on my birthday.

One time when I was a little girl, I told her about an idea I had: I wanted to have a carnival for my friends. Grandma didn't bat an eye. She set plans into motion, and before I knew it, she had filled her yard with all kinds of fun outdoor carnival games. Then we invited the neighbor kids to come, and we all had so much fun.

The sense of connection I felt to Grandma was unlike any relationship I'd ever known. When I was twelve, my family moved away from our Michigan home, where Grandma had always been just a few steps away. I missed her terribly and often wished I could transport myself across the miles, back to her house again. We made so many happy memories together. I still love thinking about her, the influence she had on me, and the joy I felt when we were together.

I wasn't shy about challenging my parents whenever I didn't agree with them. I had no interest in keeping up appearances as some kind of proof that signaled to other people how spiritual we were. And I didn't mind telling them

so. I said things none of my sisters dared to say,
which earned me the reputation of being a wild,
rebellious troublemaker. I drove my sisters crazy
because I was always stirring things up when they
would rather have let things go unsaid.

I couldn't stand the rigid rules and control my
parents wanted to have over every aspect of my
life. The anger I directed at my parents during
those teenage years was intense. I wanted them to
have my back no matter what. I longed for them to
know and care for me as a person and accept me
just as I was rather than our relationship being so
focused on what I needed to change or how I
performed. I was the only one of their four
daughters who couldn't just fall in line. I always
pushed back when something didn't feel right or
authentic. I felt mad all the time and had no
interest in trying to please my parents, unlike my
sisters. I constantly disrupted the peace whenever
I was home. Honestly, though, I was a mess.

The one outlet I had, which gave me something
positive to focus all my rage on, is that I was a

competitive athlete throughout high school. I
worked hard at whatever sport I played. My
parents loved watching from the sidelines and
always pushed me to be the best I could be. Back
then I ran at least ten miles a day and somehow
found time to be on the cheerleading squad as
well. But my favorite sport was tennis, and I
wanted to go as far as I could as a tennis player.

By my junior year of high school, my three
sisters were grown and out of the house. At that
point in our life, my dad was constantly traveling
for work and rarely ever there, which left just
Mom and me at home. I didn't want to sit around
the house feeling lonely, so I found every possible
excuse to be out doing my own thing with my
friends.

I became increasingly unhappy and even ran
away from home numerous times trying
desperately to find the connection I hungered for. I
stole an exam, trying to take a shortcut to get a
better grade, which got me suspended from high
school. Somehow, my teacher tracked me down at

Eagle Creek, a park in Indianapolis, but that stunt got me kicked off the cheerleading team. The only thing I managed to do well consistently was playing tennis.

My parents didn't know what to do with me, so they tried to get me into a boarding school for my senior year of high school, but I couldn't get in. Mom was tired of fighting with me, so she called my oldest sister to see if I could stay with her for a while. My sister had just gotten married and couldn't take me in.

During the summer before my senior year of high school, some of my friends decided to work as counselors for a Young Life camp for three months. So, I decided to do it too, because I wanted to be with my friends. And wouldn't you know, it turned out to be a life-changing experience?! I'd always hated the idea of Christianity when it all just seemed like rules against having fun. It all seemed so fake and negative. But that summer at camp, I saw a different side of faith.

I was surrounded by good people throughout that summer and found myself drawn to the kind of faith that wasn't about appearances. I found the connection I craved, not only with people but with God. That connection wasn't superficial or focused on rule-following, but it was based on the understanding that I was loved, just as I was. It wasn't about knowing all the right answers or doing everything right, but more of the kind of relationship I would have with a close friend...or my grandma.

I called a truce on all the turmoil and anger that had been brewing inside of me and decided to let all of that stuff go. My attitude changed dramatically. Those who know me might be laughing right now because I'm still feisty. I'm never going to be shy about speaking my mind. But trust me, I was a rebel and needed to make some changes for my own sanity. The decisions I made that summer began an important shift that still impacts me today.

Even still, when it came time for college, I was ready to get out from under my parents' roof and be free. I had no plans to settle down, and I was never having kids. I just wanted fun, friends, freedom, and this newly discovered version of faith I could get behind. So those were the things I pursued wholeheartedly during my first semester at Butler University.

CHAPTER THREE
SURVIVAL MODE

Scott

I would love to say that everything started looking up once I got to college, but to be honest, I struggled. After a year of college, I took a forced break. I had no money, and I didn't want to take out student loans. I knew better than to take on debt. I was determined to go back to college at some point when I had saved up some money, but for the time being, I knew I needed to find a more substantial income.

I was living with a group of buddies near the
Ball State campus in Muncie, Indiana, and would
make the ninety-minute drive down I-69 to
Indianapolis in my van multiple times each week
to look for work. Jobs in Indianapolis paid better
than those in Muncie, but it was the 1980s, and the
job market was tough.

On the drive back to Muncie after one
particularly exhausting and discouraging day of
interviews, I fell asleep at the wheel. My van hit a
guardrail alongside I-69 and rolled down an
embankment. I didn't have a seatbelt on, so my
body was ejected through the open window,
which turned out to be a blessing because my
injuries were more minor than they would have
been if I'd remained inside the vehicle as it rolled.

I miraculously walked away from that accident
with only minor injuries, but the van was totaled.
My one lifeline was that van. I had practically
been living in it at that point because I was
spending so much time in Indianapolis searching
for work.

One of my buddies in Muncie picked me up from the scene of the crash and took me back to the house. Now my need for a job was even more critical because I no longer had transportation. My body was sore and beat up from the accident, but I knew there was no time to waste.

I packed some essentials into a backpack and hitchhiked to Indianapolis to continue the increasingly desperate search for employment. I had no place to live, so late at night when most people were inside, I would find shelter in breezeways and porches of apartment buildings using my bag as a pillow. I would wake up as early as possible each morning to avoid anyone spotting me when they left for work. I did get caught a couple of times and promised people that I wouldn't come back if they didn't call the police. Then I'd have to move on to another area so I didn't get caught.

I helped clean the local YMCA part-time, which gave me access to their showers so I could clean up regularly. Meals consisted of whatever food I could find. Abandoned lunch bags with a few leftovers taste remarkably good when you are that hungry.

The thing I hungered for even more, however, was human connection. Whenever I tried to interact with people in public, many of them would ignore me altogether. Others would return disapproving expressions or tell me to go away. That was the last thing I needed at that point. I constantly felt judged by people who didn't know me, when just a little warmth or kindness would have gone a long way.

During this time, my older brother told me, "Scott, you can blame losing Mom and Dad for everything that has happened to you, and no one would blame you. Or you can let all that stuff drive you to create the kind of life you want."

He was right, of course. So, I took the skills and ability to work hard that I learned from my dad, and the prayers and love my mother had invested in me, and set out to create a better life for myself.

This was, without a doubt, the loneliest time in my life. I just wanted to be seen for who I was: a normal, hardworking kid who had been through hard times and was giving his last ounce of energy every day looking for opportunities to work toward a better future.

CHAPTER FOUR

THE START OF SOMETHING GOOD

Scott

After exhausting every job lead I could possibly explore, I was tired and discouraged. Then I got word through my sister that Dalt's, a popular upscale restaurant in Indianapolis, was hiring busboys. And she told me the bussers at Dalt's were earning more money than I had ever made up to that point. At that time, $15,000 per year sounded like a dream come true to me. So I went for it.

After three interviews and a polygraph test, I got the job. Then training began. Dalt's was part of a group of businesses that also owned Friday's and Carlson Hotels, so all the employees of those businesses went through extensive orientation and training together. Needless to say, I was anxious to get started because I had nowhere to live and no transportation. I showed up for every training no matter how difficult it was to get there because I knew this opportunity was the one I'd been waiting for to help me change my situation. I wasn't going to do anything to jeopardize it.

As soon as paychecks started coming in, I dedicated every penny I earned and every waking hour to getting money in the bank so I could find a place to live and save up for a used car for transportation. I would go to different managers and ask to pick up extra shifts, but when they realized how many hours I was working, they let me know that we were not allowed to be paid overtime.

The opportunity to earn tips on top of my hourly wage became an essential way to maximize my income. So, whenever I was scheduled to begin a shift before the restaurant opened, I would often wait to clock in until patrons started arriving at the restaurant so I could work as many hours as possible during times when I could get tips on top of the hourly wage. This way, I could increase the minimum wage to more like $20 per hour.

The staff at Dalt's was a wonderful community of people. The managers treated everyone well and, for me, that was the closest thing to having a big close family that I'd ever felt. For several of them, this was a career. And, since I was the young buck on the team, they looked out for me and taught me everything I needed to know to succeed in my job. I was eager to learn everything I could so I didn't have to face the insecurity of joblessness again.

This vivacious, friendly blonde named Nyla was a hostess, and she always knew which customers were notorious for tipping well. She would often help me out by seating the best tippers in my section. I appreciated her having my back in that way, and we got along well. Our coworkers did notice what she was doing a few times and gave her crap for it, but she didn't care a bit.

There was no romance between Nyla and me at first. In fact, I went to the hostess stand one time to ask Nyla if her sister, who also worked there, might go out with me.

"Nooo! You don't want to go out with her!" Nyla blurted out. One thing about Nyla…she never shies away from speaking her mind. She was sure her sister and I would not be a good match, so I moved on from that idea pretty quickly.

On Nyla's twenty-first birthday, she and a bunch of her friends pulled up to Dalt's in a limousine and came inside for a drink. At that point, I was growing more and more interested in Nyla. So, I nudged my buddy Kirby and told him, "We are getting in that limo before it leaves."

I'm not sure if Kirby believed me or not, but we approached the limo as soon as Nyla and her friends were all inside. I knocked on the window, and one of the girls rolled it down to see what I had to say. That's when I made my move and dove into the limo. Once I was in, Kirby quickly jumped in after me. And, just like that, we were headed down the road in a limo filled with fun, attractive young women our age.

When I jumped into the limo that night, I wasn't necessarily getting the feeling that Nyla wanted to hang out with me. So I started talking to her good friend. I kind of hoped she would feel jealous, but my plan didn't work. She assumed I was interested in her friend and kept her distance all evening. But still, I had more fun than I'd had in a long time hanging out with the group.

I had been entirely focused on surviving for so long, that it felt good to enjoy a little leisure time with people my age, especially when someone as fun and energetic as Nyla was part of the group. I was also drawn to Nyla because she was so honest and trustworthy. She didn't play games. She just said what she was thinking, which was refreshing to be around. I had never dated a girl like her. I knew she was the kind of girl who would never lie to me or cheat on me.

Soon word began to get around our work family that I was interested in Nyla. But the question remained, "Was she interested in me?"

CHAPTER FIVE

NOT JUST ANOTHER GUY

Nyla

I went to Butler University to play tennis and lived in a sorority house during my freshman year of college. I partied a lot. Maybe too much, because I didn't make high enough grades to play on the tennis team like I planned. So, I worked a lot. I taught aerobics classes in addition to working as a hostess at Dalt's so I could save money for a car. My sisters and friends also worked at Dalt's, so being together made work especially fun.

I was curious when this new employee started coming in because he was always wearing this big backpack full of things. When I first saw him, I felt bad for him. I could tell he had a lot going on, although I had no idea how much he was dealing with.

The restaurant staff was required to wear button-down shirts and a tie, and we had to have a crease down each arm of our shirts. Scott managed to get creases in his shirt every single day, somehow. I got even more curious about him when I discovered that he was using the bun steamer in the back of the kitchen to press his shirt.

I finally asked one of the servers, "What's up with this guy?" That's when I learned that Scott was sleeping on the streets.

I admired how hard he worked. I didn't know how he always looked neat and clean when he

came to work, but he was impressive. He
intrigued me, but we were not necessarily
attracted to each other at that point.

I was considered part of the "Butler elite" in
college. Even though I worked, I didn't have to
struggle to support myself like Scott did. I used
the money I earned to save for a gorgeous dark
blue Camaro rather than putting every penny into
basic survival. Scott didn't have expendable
income or free time to go out and have fun. I
admired his diligence, but we didn't hang out
much at first. Besides, I was casually seeing other
people when we first met, and I was having fun as
a wild and free college student.

He was a nice guy, so in addition to using my
position as hostess to make sure the good tippers
ended up in his section, I went to Jeffrey, the
bartender at Dalt's, to ask if he and his roommate
had any space in their apartment where Scott
could stay. He told me they had a den with a
couch, and within a couple of weeks, Scott had a
place to live. He still didn't have transportation, so

he walked everywhere he went, but at least he had a place to call home. That was a start.

A lot of our regular customers at Dalt's were nice people who were also wealthy. Some drove fancy cars like Delorians and Porches, which they would let us borrow from time to time for special occasions. One such outing happened on my twenty-first birthday, when my friends and I made our way around Indianapolis in someone's limo. That night, when Scott and Kirby jumped into the limo through the open window, we had fun, but I thought he was interested in my friend. I had no idea he was interested in me.

After that night, Scott started teasing me because one of the guys I'd been dating casually was playing in the Final Four. He told me if this guy's team won the Final Four, I had to take Scott out on a date. And if the guy's team lost, Scott got to take me out. It was a pretty sneaky bet, because either way, he was getting a date out of the deal, and I was driving because he didn't have a car.

Well, the guy lost. So Scott asked me out. The plan was for us to have dinner at a popular seafood restaurant. I wasn't excited about the date at first. Scott showed up in these tight white pants, which I later teased him about, but by the time we pulled into the restaurant parking lot, we were so deep in conversation that neither of us opened our door to go inside. That was when Scott finally told me his story. He told me about running home to help his mom during the tornado when he was nine, about losing his father to cancer, the financial struggles, how he took care of his mom until she died, living by himself, the van accident, and how determined he was to get back on his feet.

I'd always heard that if you want to know how a man will treat you, watch how he treats his mother. I knew the way Scott devoted himself to his mom's well-being at such a young age was rare, and I was moved by that. I mean, if a teenager is helping his mom with her catheter, he is a pretty rare human being. I knew this wasn't the kind of guy who would abandon me, and I didn't know any other guys like that. There was a respect there that I'd never had for anyone else I dated.

We never even made it into the restaurant that night. When I heard his story and better understood his situation, I didn't want him to buy me dinner. Instead, we sat out in the car talking for more than two hours. There were some things about Scott I wasn't sure about at that point, but regardless, after that date, I said to myself, "I could marry him."

CHAPTER SIX

A TERRIBLE END TO A DATE

Scott

I, too, walked away from our first date thinking, "I could marry her." We were so young and in very different places in life. I was serious and focused on surviving, so every moment of my time was spent working to get myself into a better position financially. Getting a place to live and transportation would take time and a lot of sacrifice.

I watched how great Nyla was with people at the hostess desk. She was like a magnet. She just drew people in and she was a lot of fun. I knew, for the time being, I had a great friend in her.

I not only enjoyed being around her, but I also could tell there was a lot more to her than meets the eye at first. She was not just a fun girl with well-off parents. She had integrity. She was loyal and didn't turn her back on her friends. I had been figuring things out alone for so long, that I longed for more of that kind of friendship in my life. So we started spending more and more time together, usually in group settings.

One late-summer weekend, I got into the driver's seat of Nyla's dark blue Camaro to drive her and two of her sorority sisters from Indianapolis to Cincinnati for a preseason Bengals football game. We stopped for gas on the way out of Indianapolis, then I did a U-turn in a construction zone on Post Road to get over to the interstate, which happened to be a no-U-turn zone. I immediately saw police lights in my rearview mirror, and my heart sank.

When the officer walked up to the window and asked for the license and registration, I gave the officer my driver's license and the registration for Nyla's Camaro. The officer went back to check my license against his database before issuing the ticket, but soon he was back at my window informing me there was a warrant out for my arrest.

My heart sank. This was the last thing in the world I needed. Turns out, I hadn't shown up for a court date after rolling the van a few months earlier. Although I had no vehicle to get to court, no phone number or address, and I couldn't afford a day off or a taxi to show up for that court hearing, I knew I had to accept the consequences.

Our weekend date ended with me being handcuffed, escorted to the backseat of a police car, and taken directly to Marion County Jail.

Nyla was bewildered. I'm sure she wondered what else she didn't know about me.

When the police drove off with me, Nyla's sorority sisters looked at her and asked, "Who is this guy?! Who are you dating?!"

In addition to being a fun, well-liked person, Nyla was from a conservative Christian home. She volunteered for Young Life, was involved in a church community, and actively modeled her life after Jesus. She believed in the power of prayer and spent more time praying during a typical week than I'd spent praying in years.

I was a vagabond who used to go to Catholic mass with my mom as a kid until she got too sick to attend. I was not actively thinking about spiritual things at all. When out of the blue I got arrested and put behind bars, I figured, "Why *wouldn't* someone with her values be concerned about my character?!"

The county jail was terrifying. I was placed in a cell with thirty or forty other people, several of whom looked like they might pick a fight with me at any moment. So I kept to myself and tried not to do anything that would draw anyone's attention. There were open toilets shared by everyone in the cell, and there was no way I was going to let this crowd watch me go to the bathroom. I somehow managed to hold it for the next three days.

Regardless of Nyla's concerns, she went to her parents and explained my situation, begging them to use their connections to help me. As you might imagine, her request did not create the ideal first impression of his daughter's new boyfriend. But in true Nyla style, when she cares about something, she will not take "no" for an answer. Her dad happened to be playing golf with his attorney in Indianapolis and agreed to see what he could do.

This certainly was not how I planned on making my first impression on her family. I had no idea that she would go to bat for me the way she did. Nyla had plenty of other friends and I'm sure lots of guys would have been thrilled to go out with her. She didn't *have* to do what she did, but I

am grateful for the way she responded to that
terrible end to what was supposed to be a fun day
together.

CHAPTER SEVEN
A LITTLE HELP
Nyla

My father was already not thrilled with me for not doing well at Butler. So you can imagine how it went over when I asked him to help this guy I liked because he was in jail. At first, he was furious and he refused.

"Dad, I really love this guy. He is a good person. He deserves a chance," I pleaded.

I hadn't even told Scott that I loved him yet. But, by this time, I did. Dad could see that this was

important to me, and he eventually came around.
He had a conversation with his friend, the
attorney, and agreed to meet with Scott.

Even under the strange circumstances, Dad
was surprised at how well Scott presented himself
— clean, well-groomed, smart — which was
important to him. Scott walked into this meeting
with Dad and his attorney directly from the cell
he'd shared with dozens of other people for the
past three days, and though he was still wearing
the shirt he had on when we set off for the
Cincinnati Bengals game, he turned it inside out
so the shirt appeared clean and fresh.

My dad could see right away the same quality
about Scott that I saw. Yes, he was a twenty-one-
year-old kid struggling in life, but he was trying to
get on a better path with no resources and
minimal support. He was doing everything in his
power to try to get his life on track, he just needed
someone to advocate for him.

Fortunately, the attorney was able to help Scott
and he was released from jail that very day. After

everything Scott had been through, I knew he
deserved to have someone go to bat for him. He
was grateful to my dad for giving him a chance.

After that ordeal, Scott could see that I was
serious about wanting to support him. But we
were still not aligned spiritually. That would be a
dealbreaker for me. Yet we both knew we wanted
to be together.

One evening not long after his stint in jail, Scott
and I sat together on my parents' porch talking.
He had observed what my faith meant to me and
knew he needed divine help to grow into the
person he wanted to be. He had tried life on his
own, and it hadn't worked out that great. So, that
night, he told me that he finally understood that
trusting in a Source greater than himself was a
step he needed to take. We held hands and said a
prayer together right then and there. He had
always been a good person and a man of integrity,
and he always took responsibility for his mistakes.
But that night, he chose to entrust his life and
future to God.

CHAPTER EIGHT

ONWARD & UPWARD

Scott

My mom and I had spiritual conversations when I was young, and I often went with her to mass. But my decision to follow Christ that night was the beginning of a relearning process for me. Nyla prayed about everything but I'd always just pulled myself up by the bootstraps and powered

through all the struggles and setbacks I faced. I
will always be a person who is wired to take
action and do what needs to be done, so learning
to lean on God's wisdom, to have faith that goes
beyond myself, and to participate in a church
community became increasingly important for me.

I knew, when I got the job at Dalt's, that I had
finally an opportunity to improve my situation.
This was my chance to create a better life for
myself. I knew how to work hard and would do
whatever I needed to do to succeed, and that is
exactly what I did. Work came naturally to me.

My hard work was recognized by my
managers and soon I was moved from bussing
tables to server. Within a short time, I became the
head server. Nyla's hard work was also rewarded
with a promotion, and she became a corporate
trainer at the age of twenty. Things seemed to be
coming together for us.

Though I was growing professionally, I was
also growing closer to God and to Nyla. She and I
adopted a simple illustration back then that

represents how important our spiritual lives became in our relationship with one another. Picture a triangle with Nyla at the bottom of one corner, me at the bottom of the other corner, and God at the top corner. The closer each of us moved toward God, the closer we naturally drew to each other.

We were dating pretty seriously when she had to leave town for about eight weeks to train the staff of a new Dalt's location that was about to open in New York. Several other members of our Indianapolis team also went to training events like these with Nyla, including Jeff, the bartender who let me rent space in his apartment.

We were all friends and all working hard trying to get on our feet. One buddy of mine gave me rides home from work when he realized I was walking to work every day. I even walked to the restaurant through a snowstorm that shut down a lot of the city. Nothing was going to keep me from showing up. I knew what it was like to not have

anything or anyone to fall back on, and I was
never going to jeopardize my job.

By the time I turned 22, I was promoted to
management. I was flown to Dallas the following
week to attend management training, and I was,
by far, the youngest person in the management
training program. I didn't feel that young since I'd
been living on my own since before I turned
sixteen. Regardless of my youth, I was serious
about learning everything I could about how to
manage a restaurant.

When I got back into town, I got some awful
news. I was informed that Nyla would no longer
be able to work at Dalt's because managers were
not allowed to date employees. I had no intention
of my promotion impacting her. Thankfully, the
executives wanted to retain us both, so they
offered Nyla a position at one of the other
locations within their business network. She
became a concierge at the Raddison, which she
loved. It was a great fit for her personality, and she
was a natural at helping people. She ended up

being really happy with the change, which was a relief.

We took a Spring Break trip to Virginia Beach in May of 1984, a week that proved to be monumental for a few reasons. Nyla and I were spending as much time together as possible, our careers were trending upward, and we were finally on the same page spiritually. I was feeling more hopeful about the future than ever.

The more time we spent together, the more our attraction and connection to one another intensified. We knew we loved each other and began to talk openly about wanting to be together forever. At only twenty-one and twenty-two years old, we had a lot of dreams and things we wanted to accomplish, but by the end of that spring, we knew without a doubt that we wanted to pursue those things together.

CHAPTER NINE
CURVEBALL

Nyla

I'm pregnant. I didn't mince words with Scott. I never do.

I had been in denial for weeks, but I'd finally gotten confirmation from the doctor. Since I was an athlete who ran multiple miles every day, I'd been telling myself that I was missing periods because I was so physically active. But I could only avoid the truth for so long. Scott was surprised, but immediately responded in a way that brought relief.

"Okay! This isn't how we saw things going, but we know we want to be together. So let's get married! We'll just move up the timeline!"

I dreaded telling my parents I was pregnant, so I held off saying anything for as long as possible. They knew Scott and I were planning to get married and I had even scheduled a shopping day to look at wedding dresses with my mom, but given their conservative Christian viewpoints, I knew they would have a fit.

The day we went to pick out my wedding dress, Mom looked at my belly in the dress. That's when she knew. I was twelve weeks along by this time and too skinny everywhere else to conceal the baby bump that was growing more evident every day.

Mom's demeanor immediately changed, and she made it clear to me that this wedding was going to look very different than the one we had been planning. I wasn't going to get married in a church, but rather in my parents' living room. And we would not be inviting hundreds of friends from the community, church, and country club. It would be just the four of us. Scott and I, Mom, and Dad.

I called one of my three older sisters, hoping for a little support, but she called me a derogatory name and hung up on me. The friction with my side of the family didn't last forever but, once again, I was the daughter who didn't play by the rules. Having their affection withheld was the penance I had to pay because I had caused them shame by getting pregnant before marriage.

Regardless, at the end of the day on November 16, 1984, Scott and were married. Of all the choices we've made that could be called into question, marrying each other is one decision we are glad we made. Not that we haven't had days, weeks, or months when things got dicey, but at the end of the day, we know we are better together than apart.

Rather than the $25,000 wedding my sister got a few years earlier, we received $2500 from my parents to help with the cost of having a baby. We couldn't take a honeymoon because that money all needed to go for hospital bills and necessities. All we could afford was a simple band for an engagement ring, which I didn't care about at all. We got matching bands from Walmart.

My parents offered to take us to Chicago after the wedding, which was a three-hour drive north.

Wedding Day - November 16, 1984

We took them up on it because that was the only way would be able to get out of town.

We probably walked ten miles through the streets of Chicago that weekend just to have time together without my parents. Even though I was six months pregnant at this point, we walked from our downtown hotel to the stadium and back. That walk was our best honeymoon memory.

One of my sisters was married and pregnant during the same time I was. So she made sure I knew that she wanted to use the name Ansley if she had a girl. I loved that name, but she was pretty sure she was having a girl and I was told that I was having a boy. So that settled that.

A few months later, she gave birth to a boy. Then, on February 10, 1985, I had a girl. I named her Ashley so my sister could use the name Ansley if her next child was a girl.

I did not talk to the sister who hung up on me for at least five months. She left the country on a mission trip to the red-light district of Amsterdam and was still there when I gave birth. During that trip, she got to know some women that she might once have thought less of because of their choices. After learning their stories, she seemed to soften toward me. One day she called my mom to check on me and she asked Mom if my baby had been born yet.

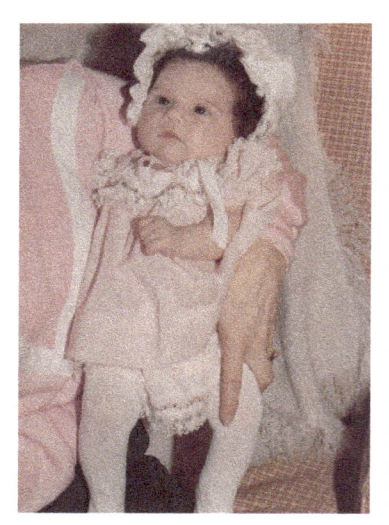

"Yes, she had a baby girl…on your birthday," Mom told her. Things were different with my sister after that. We ended up becoming closer than we had ever been before.

I remember feeling so lost as a new mother. I was going to be a career woman who traveled, went places with friends, and had things to look forward to. This wasn't at all what I had envisioned for my life. Kids had never been part of my plan.

Scott and I just owned one car between us, so he would leave for work every morning and I would be home alone with this baby and no car until he returned in the evening. He worked long days, as most people in the restaurant industry do, so I spent the majority of my time alone with a newborn.

I have never considered myself an overly religious person, and I was far too bold and free-spirited to see myself as a subservient, compliant wife who was content to stay home while her husband made a living. I quickly realized I could not survive this season of life on my own.

We joined a church community and got involved there, which was good. But I was still lonely during the long days at home. So, I began to talk to the only friend I could. I taped a picture of Jesus to the wall in my closet and went there often to talk to him. I would cry, yell, beg for

strength, and unload all of the worries I was
carrying on Him.

Our apartment was tiny, so we stored a small
collection of Scott's childhood memorabilia in a
storage unit a few miles down the road. He didn't
have much in the way of material possessions
from his childhood after losing his parents, but he
had a few trophies from wrestling, baby books
with his mom's handwriting, as well as photos
and newspaper articles about his football and
wrestling victories. Since money was so tight, we
couldn't always make timely payments to the
storage unit. After a few months, we saved up as
much as we could to try retrieving Scott's boxes
only to learn that the manager thought we had
abandoned the unit. He had taken all of the
memorabilia from Scott's childhood to the
dumpster. To this day, we only have one photo of
Scott as a baby. His siblings swear it isn't even
him, but I believe it is him.

Those first years together were tough, but
living within our means was far more important to

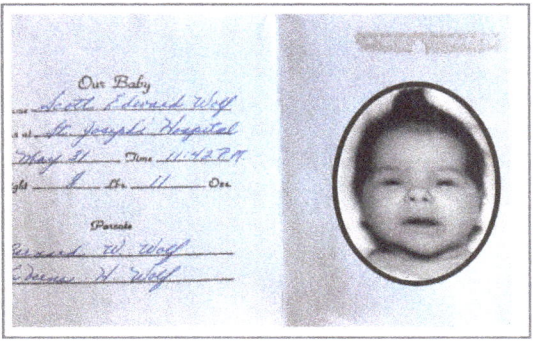

Scott's only baby photo

us than having stuff. That is one thing that has never changed about us throughout the years.

As our baby girl grew, being a mom brought me more joy than I expected. We used a giant '80s video camera to record her cooing, learning to eat, and responding as we called her name, "Ashley, can you say 'mama?'"

She was less than a year old when my sister told me that she would not be having any more kids and would not be using the name Ansley. So, I went to the local courthouse and filed the paperwork to change her name from Ashley to

Grandma & Grandpa Peelen with "Ashley"
(before her name was Ansley)

Ansley. I knew I had to do it before she turned one year old, so for only ten dollars, I had her name legally changed just three months before her first birthday.

Our family still dies laughing when we watch those old family videos hear our voices calling her Ashley!

CHAPTER TEN

STARTING A BUSINESS

Scott

Not long after Ansley was born, two local businessmen approached me while I was managing Dalt's, handed me a business card, and asked me to give them a call about an opportunity they had for me to open a new restaurant. I shrugged them off, not really thinking they were serious. Pretty soon, they stopped by again.

"You never called," they said. I explained that I didn't really think they were serious.

They went on to explain that they owned a club in a prime location at Keystone at the Crossing that they wanted to turn into a fine dining location. That location was an up-and-coming area of Indianapolis at the time.

I agreed to help them develop and build the restaurant, and then run it. But I was clear with them that I hadn't done anything quite like this before. So they brought in a guy from Boston with extensive experience building high-end restaurants who worked with me to build a great restaurant from the ground up. But they wanted me to build it.

I still, to this day, marvel at why they sought me out to do this. It was an opportunity I never imagined having, but I went *all in*. Ansley was a baby, Nyla and I were still in our early twenties, and I was being trusted to build, open, and manage the Keystone Grill in Indianapolis. This restaurant went on to become an award-winning seafood and steak restaurant that was considered the best in Indianapolis for years, but I would spend seventy or eighty hours a week building it.

That project was an incredible opportunity and I found that kind of work was a good fit for my skills and personality. When Keystone Grill opened in 1986, Nyla was about to deliver our second child, Alec. We had bought a little house in Indianapolis and I was grateful for what I had been able to accomplish, but with our second child on the way and seeing how hard it was for Nyla to basically parent without me most of the time, I knew the pace I was keeping was unsustainable if I was going to have the kind of marriage and family that I wanted.

A great friend and mentor of mine, Pat Kirk, offered me the opportunity to become the GM for a more casual restaurant called Charley & Barney's, which wasn't open as late and would not require the long hours I was keeping at Keystone Grill. So I took that opportunity.

Alec and Ansley circa summer of 1987

While I worked for Charley and Barney's, Nyla and I moved to a slightly bigger house down the street that gave us more space and a bigger yard that would accommodate our growing family. By this time, we had a second car so Nyla could take the kids places. I had learned a lot about how to run a profitable restaurant, and life was stable.

After serving as the general manager at Charlie and Barney's for about two years, an entrepreneurial friend of mine invited me to start a business with him. He put up a $25,000 loan as a

silent partner and we formed the AAA Railroad
Tie company, which I would run. It wasn't
restaurant work, but it required business savvy
and hard work, and tapped into my creativity,
which I enjoyed. The business plan involved
salvaging railroad ties and installing them for
various uses such as landscape designs for
individuals and businesses.

We were based out of Whitestown, Indiana,
but one of our first jobs was an installation for a
lady who lived off the fairway of Crooked Stick
golf course in Carmel. We built a series of railroad
tie boxes around the back of her home, which she
had landscapers turn into a series of stunning
garden boxes. Not long after that installation, Pete
Dye, one of the most famous golf course
developers in North America, saw this lady's yard
from the Crooked Stick fairway and proceeded to
drive his golf cart up to her back door to ask her
who installed the garden boxes in her yard.

Pretty soon after that, I got a call from Pete
Dye, asking if I could give him a bid for an

installation at the number-one tee box at Crooked
Stick. This was in 1988, and Crooked Stick was
slated to host the PGA Championship in 1991, so
Pete hired AAA to do an installation on the
number one tee box.

Pleased with the outcomes, Pete continued to
hire AAA for railroad tie installations across the
entire golf course during the two years leading up
to the PGA Championship. One of those projects
was a bridge, which remains a defining feature of
the Crooked Stick golf course to this day.

After a couple of years of working alongside
the Crooked Stick landscapers and foremen, we
were working on the bridge when I commented to
one of the guys on the landscape crew about the
older guy working with us.

"That guy is funny, and man does he ever
know his shit!" I gushed.

My buddy on the crew informed me that this
funny older guy was Pete Dye, who had been
signing my checks for nearly three years. I had
talked to him on the phone but never realized we

had been working shoulder-to-shoulder in the trenches to bring his vision for the course to life.

Working on the bridge at Crooked Stick

I wasn't a golfer before the Crooked Stick project, and I wasn't familiar with Pete before that time, but I got to know him and his wife, Alice, during the years that followed. Pete and Alice took me in like family, and I learned a great deal from them.

One day when I was visiting their home, Alice and I were talking about how Pete always wore

The finished bridge at Crooked Stick Golf
Course

khakis and white shirts. I'd noticed this about him
but never asked until it came up during this
conversation. Alice then walked me back to his
closet and I couldn't believe what I saw. White
shirts and khaki pants filled the closet. Then she
disclosed the secret of why I never saw him
wearing anything else. She told me that he was
constantly bombarded with decisions all day,
every day. But wearing the same thing each day
meant there was one decision he never had to
worry about making. This is the kind of practical

man he is, and I have learned a great deal from his unique perspective on life and business.

When the time came for the PGA Championship, Pete gave me a gold badge that would allow me free VIP access to the entire event. I never saw the big picture of what we'd been working on until I saw how it all played out during that weekend. Watching the players competing on the course while television cameras rolled, I could see how every single bunker and design choice Pete had made throughout the previous three years made perfect sense.

That weekend also revealed to me the level of Pete's influence. He was so down-to-earth that it took me watching him in action to fully understand what an opportunity he had given me to work on this project.

After finishing Crooked Stick, Pete invited me to help him build the Brickyard in Indianapolis. By this time, I understood the kind of man I was working for. Together, we embarked on that project, and he seemed to have a lot more work in the pipeline.

At this point, my original business partner wanted to move on to other things, so I bought him out of his share of the landscape company and became the sole owner of AAA Landscaping. I was just twenty-five years old at this point and we had two kids at home.

When the Brickyard project was coming to an end, Pete approached me with the opportunity of a lifetime. He invited me to install railroad ties at the rest of his golf courses across the United States. This would mean business and exposure indefinitely! I couldn't wait to tell Nyla the big news.

When I told her about about Pete's offer, I was shocked at her response.

"Hell no!" she insisted. "Absolutely not."

"Are you serious?! Do you understand that we will be set for life if I do this? I will never have to bid for another job again!"

Then I thought about it and I understood exactly why Nyla didn't want me to pursue this opportunity. I would be traveling all over the country, away from our two young children and her. I knew her dad was always traveling and never around when she was a kid and I didn't want to do that to her or the kids.

When she was growing up, Nyla would have easily given up being dropped off at school in a Mercedes or having fancy dinners at the country club if she could have traded those things for a close relationship with her father. She had seen first-hand what happens when someone is married to his work instead of being engaged and present for his family.

When I thought about this opportunity from that perspective, I knew she was right. I didn't want to sacrifice our connection as a couple or with our kids for the business. So, I declined Pete's offer. I'm pretty sure he had never been turned down before, and I hated to disappoint him. But my family was more important.

Ansley and Alec playing at AAA

CHAPTER ELEVEN

FACING OUR MOUNTAIN

Scott

AAA was doing okay, and I was having fun, but a couple of companies we were doing big projects for ran up large bills then stopped paying their invoices. We had a line of credit we used to make up-front purchases for large jobs, and we had hours and hours of labor tied up in those projects. But when we tried to collect from the first company that owed us, we were notified that they had filed for bankruptcy, and we would not be recovering any of the money they owed. That was a huge hit.

The truth is, I'd gotten out of my realm with this company. I understood the restaurant business. I had fun with the landscaping work, but I didn't fully understand how to make money in the landscaping business. I wasn't charging enough to provide the necessary margin to manage the massive cost of supplies and equipment. So not getting paid for the costs or labor of that large project was devastating.

Three or four months later, a second company that owed us thousands of dollars also filed for bankruptcy. Upon learning that the second client would also not be paying their invoices after all the costs we incurred on credit, I knew immediately we would not be able to recover.

I called Nyla and told her that AAA Landscaping was done. We would have to sell as much equipment and inventory as possible to pay off the line of credit. But, even after trying to recover some of the lost funds, we could barely touch the astronomical amount we owed. With every month that passed, interest on that debt and estimated taxes accrued until our total debt had snowballed into around $300,000 within a few months.

We began making moves to turn the landscaping company into a wholesale nursery and retail garden market so we could get cash coming in again to start working off the debt. We sold trucks and began moving the remaining inventory from Whitestown, Indiana, to Hillsdale Garden Center north of Indianapolis, where a landlord in the Castleton area had a building we could rent.

Even after making that move, I soon realized we weren't going to make enough money to pay the debt while also supporting our family.

Then came the hardest part. I sat down with Nyla and told her, "Honey, we can get through this. But it is going to be really hard for a while. We need to sell the house and one of the cars, and I'm going to need you to manage Hillsdale so I can go back to work full-time."

That conversation went about like you would expect, at first. She was devastated. But we sold everything and signed the lease to rent a tiny one-bedroom condo with a loft in a rundown neighborhood.

I didn't want to do to our creditors what had been done to us. We wanted to do right by our lenders. And I knew if we filed for bankruptcy, our creditors would recover maybe ten cents on the dollar of what we owed them. So I met with each of our creditors and agreed not to file for bankruptcy if they would stop the accrual of interest and penalties. That would give us the best opportunity to pay off the entire amount we owed within our lifetime. They all agreed eventually.

Meanwhile, my buddies who were managers and GMs when I worked at Dalt's kept telling me about this new hot place called Applebee's where they were all working.

"Wolfie, this place is hot, it's growing, you've gotta get in on this," they convinced me.

I needed to start working again, and Applebee's had three restaurants in Indianapolis. So, I interviewed for a manager position at one of their locations and got the job. Then we began the long climb toward financial recovery the only way you can conquer any mountain…one step at a time.

CHAPTER TWELVE
HILLSDALE
Nyla

I was shocked at how quickly our life went from being *really* good to losing everything. I had never had to struggle financially like that in my life. I was angry with God and angry with Scott for letting the business fail, plus I was feeling sorry for myself about everything we had lost.

It all came to a head during an intense argument between Scott and me. I was complaining about how bad our circumstances were and how I didn't want to sell our house and have to live in a tiny, drab condo. I was having a huge pity party, but then something Scott said stopped me in my tracks.

"Do you think I wanted my parents to die?"

His words hung in the air. That was when the reality hit me that I had never faced anything this hard. But Scott had made it through much harder circumstances than this. And he had to do that without anyone by his side to support him.

Hillsdale before we moved the business there

I knew I needed to get over myself and stop acting like a princess so I could see Scott through this and become part of the solution. We were in this together and I knew how to work hard. So I knew we could make it through this, but we had to do it together.

The day we had to vacate our house, we could not put a deposit down on the rented condo until we got Scott's Applebee's paycheck the next day. We had no money for a hotel and no place to spend the night before we could move into to the condo.

No one in our life knew how bad things were, so I didn't feel like I could ask anyone, not even my parents, if we could stay with them overnight. We didn't even have enough money for a hotel. So we told the kids we were going camping. We slept in our car that night and pretended we were on an adventure so Ansley and Alec wouldn't be afraid or worried.

The next morning we would move into a one-bedroom loft condo. We were barely moved in when the police started knocking on our door regularly to serve papers about the money we owed. I was terrified that they might conclude from our empty cupboards and sparse living conditions that we were not fit parents and send CPS to the house. To ramp up that fear even more, our neighbor took an immediate dislike to the kids and me. She was rude to us and even left mean notes on our car.

The landlord was sweet, even though I often had to run rent checks over in person just in the nick of time. However, I hated living in that condo. I looked forward to getting up at 5:00 each morning and going to work just to get out of that place.

I would bring the kids with me early to help pick corn or load pumpkins into our truck to sell at our market. I'd take them to school before heading over to Hillsdale, where I would spend the day selling produce and plants, driving the Bobcat, moving railroad ties, and loading mulch and landscape supplies into clients' trucks. And wouldn't you know, I ended up loving it. I have a lot of good memories of that time.

Our building was nothing more than a pole barn with no heat or bathrooms. The one thing we did have in abundance was raccoons. One day Alec went out back to get a box of produce and came running back into the garden center to let me (and everyone within earshot) know there was a raccoon back there! I tried to quiet him down so the customers weren't scared off, but when no one was watching I'd disappear to go run the raccoons off to keep them out of our inventory.

The kids were an important part of the team at Hillsdale, and running the business became a family project. Alec went to his first day of kindergarten with mud on his shirt and bragged to all his friends that he had already unloaded a truck full of pumpkins before school started. He thought it was cool that he had a job where he got dirty before he showed up to school.

Ansley was a little older, so she would ask us to drop her off around the corner so none of her classmates would see her getting out of a truck filled with pumpkins or corn. But she was equally helpful and learned skills other kids her age didn't have, like how to speak to customers and give them the correct change when they paid in cash.

Hillsdale after we got it up and running

My team consisted of my sister, my cousin, my kids, and Scott. Turned out my cousin was quite good at driving a Bobcat. She was also single and trying to meet people. She had her eye on a certain landscaper who came in regularly, and she wanted to meet him. So whenever he showed up, she'd

Ansley and Alec "staying on top of things" at Hillsdale.

secretly put on lipstick before going out to help him, hoping he would notice her. One day, while she was helping this handsome landscaper load mulch into his truck, a gust of wind came along and blew the mulch into her face causing her lipstick to serve as glue for the mulch. I'm sure the lipstick got his attention, but not in the way she hoped. We never let her live that down.

There were so many fun moments like that at Hillsdale. We worked hard and built it into a happening place. Things were not easy for us to say the least, but we also experienced a lot of joy working together as a family.

During the winter, we sold around 1,500 Christmas trees, and at other times of year we sold produce or whatever was in season at the time. Hillsdale became an iconic place in the Indianapolis area, and the business did well. With everyone pitching in to help, we kept it going strong for about ten years.

The one thing about our life that brought the most stress was our housing situation. Our tiny one-bedroom loft condo was oppressive, and apartment living didn't feel safe for the kids to be able to play. I longed to be able to look out our windows and see something beautiful.

As I'd done so many times before, I began to pray. I begged God for a better housing situation. My sister encouraged me to write down what I envisioned and to be specific. So I started praying for a house like Little House on the Prairie with space around it, a pretty environment, and a long driveway with a tree in the yard.

Before long, I got a call from my sister who had just learned about a house for rent in Noblesville for $650 per month. For that kind of rent, I imagined the place would be awful, but when we drove up to the address, we followed a long driveway along the property of a historic village called Conner Prairie, which is surrounded by fields and green space. Not only was the house everything I prayed for, but "prairie" was even in

Little House on Conner Prairie

the name of the village where the house was
located! It was just the miracle I needed to know
we would get through this.

I sold the wedding ring Scott had bought me
during the days when AAA was going well, which
helped cover the first couple of months of rent. We
moved in to the house as quickly as possible to get
out of that cramped apartment.

Scott was working for Applebee's corporate at
this point, so we finally began to make some
headway on the debt while we lived in our "little
house on the prairie" for the next five years.
During those years, we had unlimited access to the
beautiful historic village and even enjoyed
weekend fireworks shows from our lawn during
Symphony on the Prairie every weekend during
the summer.

Those years running were a turning point in
our life, our marriage, and my faith. We would
probably still live there today if they hadn't turned
that house into a conference center a few years
later. We loved living there, and I still look back

with gratitude for those years when we were doing everything we could to solve our situation and saw our prayers answered in such a specific and personal way.

Christmas photo at the Conner Prairie house.

CHAPTER THIRTEEN

BUILDING A FUTURE

Scott

Something unexpected was happening over at Hillsdale. While I was working all day and no longer able to help with daily operations, Nyla and her sister and cousins were running Bobcats, hauling railroad ties, and lifting mulch into customers' trucks. If something stopped working, Nyla would say a prayer over it, bang on it a couple of times, and usually get it working again! Customers apparently enjoyed having beautiful women help them with their landscaping supplies because Hillsdale started doing well without me there.

I would come by after work to help clean up things for the night and our kids were always there helping Nyla. I realized then that if I had taken Pete up on his offer to travel the United States and do installations on all his golf courses, we would never have had the opportunity to work together like this.

Even though we were not yet where we wanted to be from a stability perspective, I look back with gratitude for a wife and family who jumped in and helped us with what seemed like an insurmountable mountain of debt to overcome. We were in it together. That is the only way I ever want to face adversity — together.

Everything Nyla and I have ever done was for our family. We didn't make money or start businesses to get rich or to achieve a certain lifestyle. At first, it was about survival. We did whatever was necessary to get on our feet and get out of debt.

It seemed to take forever, but we worked our way out of crisis mode after more than ten years. When we knew we would not be able to keep renting the house on Conner Prairie anymore, we we had to look for something more permanent.

We were grateful that the years of hard work were dwindling down the debt significantly so we could begin focusing more on building stability.

The fixer-upper before renovation.

We wanted to incorporate what each of us had learned growing up and create family memories together like Nyla and her grandmother did, while also providing financial stability and opportunities for the future.

I haven't talked about my dad much, and I only knew him for the first fifteen years of my life, but he showed me how to build and fix things. He always had projects going, including a small cabin at the lake that he fixed up, and he brought my siblings and me in on those projects to help him. I learned to do all kinds of carpentry jobs and repairs as a kid, which eventually helped me with the restaurants I built. Anytime repairs, renovations, or upgrades were needed, I had the skills to do most of them myself.

When we learned about an old house for sale that sat on a piece of land out in the country in Noblesville, I was interested. We knew we had to move out of the house at Conner Prairie by a certain date, so I went to take a look. It was in rough shape and needed a lot of work. There was no electricity, and it needed to be completely refurbished inside and out, but it was located on a great piece of land with a lot of potential. Because of the condition of the house, the price was low. So, we bought it, and I began fixing it up during whatever spare hours I could find between working at Applebees and helping Nyla build the Hillsdale business.

We moved into the fixer-upper in 1996 and felt so blessed to have a nice home with space around it just like Nyla had been dreaming about since before we moved to the Conner Prairie home… only this house belonged to us.

We had visions of buying the land around it in the future. We imagined our kids building homes on the surrounding acreage and even pictured grandkids running around on the hills around it someday. But this was what we could do for now, and we were incredibly grateful.

CHAPTER FOURTEEN
NYLA'S
Nyla

After about 10 years at Hillsdale, we got the opportunity to rent a space in downtown Noblesville. The landlord at Hillsdale needed us to move because Lowe's was looking at building a store on his property. We had a good relationship with the landlord of Hillsdale, and even talked about opening a second Hillsdale location at the Noblesville building, but he didn't want us to take the name with us.

Back when I was in college, I had taken a business class and registered a business name as part of an assignment. The business name was: "Nyla's: Best Between New York & LA" so we went with that for the name of this new place in Noblesville. We were able to move to the new location under that new name quickly and easily since I had already registered it.

Nyla's was originally a garden center and cafe, but the only items on the menu were coffee and homemade pastries called kringles. We started selling the kringles during the Christmas season using a small kitchen in the back of the building. People loved being able to have coffee and pastries while they shopped. During weekends throughout the season, we would easily sell 200 of them per day.

The only problem was that it took three days to produce a batch of these pastries. Each one had 144 layers, which required a labor-intensive process that included kneading, and more kneading. It was a lot of work, but there were so many great memories made there, too.

We opened at 7:00 in the morning, closed at 2:00 in the afternoon, and we were open seven days a week. We spent every evening making huge batches of pastries for the next morning, then I would get about four or five hours of sleep before we were up and at it again the next day.

We could see that even the simple, two-item menu of coffee and kringles was quickly becoming more popular than plants, trees, or garden supplies. People would stand in long lines for these kringles, and our profits were going up as a result. So, I started to wonder what other food items we could offer, keeping in mind that I am not a cook.

Scott was a general manager for Applebee's at this point, so I asked him if they had any old equipment they weren't using. He found a flattop grill they wanted to get rid of, and I figured I could at least flip an egg. How hard could that be? So, I turned Nyla's into a breakfast place.

I'll be honest, at first I was pretty bad at it. My omelets all came out all different sizes and I had no idea what I was doing. But I kept at it and used that flattop grill to keep trying new items. After offering breakfast only for about a year, I added wraps and sandwiches, and word started spreading in the community that Nyla's was a good place to come for breakfast and lunch.

I decided to homeschool Alec for a year, and he learned to be a line cook at Nyla's that year. Other than that, I am honestly not sure what else I taught him. He attended a co-op class with some other homeschooled kids on Tuesdays and Thursdays, and the other three days of the week were up to me. He remembers police officers stopping him when he went outside to empty the trash, and they asked him why he wasn't in school. When he told them he was homeschooled, they came inside to ask me for the paperwork as proof. Or maybe they followed the smell of the kringles. Either way, Alec says that was his favorite year of school, but I'm pretty sure I did it so he could help me at the restaurant. We still laugh about it because I'm the least likely homeschool mom you will ever meet.

After being in business for about a year and a half, I got a call from an attorney who informed me that Britney Spears wanted to use the restaurant name, "Nyla's: Best Between New York and LA" (only the "LA" would stand for Lousiana, instead of Los Angelos). Since I had already registered the name, Britney couldn't legally use it unless we were willing to give it up.

Our lawyers went back and forth for the next few months. I was not going to give up the name. The business was starting to grow and we had too much at stake to start over under a different name. Britney either had to change her restaurant name or buy our restaurant. In the end, we were able to continue operating as Nyla's and Britney had to choose another restaurant name. In the end, she severed ties with the restaurant in late 2002.

Soon, after everything was resolved, I walked into the cafe to be greeted by a life-sized cardboard cutout of Spears with my face on it.

Some of my regulars had snuck it in as a joke, and we all had a good laugh. I'm pretty sure I still have that cutout in storage somewhere.

Running a garden center taught us that the one thing we could make money on was food. Who knew? It wasn't what we planned, but we couldn't ignore a line of people wrapped around the building. So we added to the menu. Becoming a restaurant was never part of the plan for Nyla's, but like everything we did, we went with the flow and kept riding the waves.

About the time money started coming in at Nyla's, Scott was promoted again and became a franchise consultant for Applebee's. His job required a lot of traveling and the kids were getting older, so Scott was not as involved in the operations at Nyla's simply because there wasn't time.

One weekend he decided to check in on the books for Nyla's. Whenever he started poking around and asking questions about the books, I would get defensive. I was working day and night to make it all happen while also making sure the kids were okay, and I didn't want him looking over my shoulder.

Keeping track of expenses and paperwork is his strong suit. And he knows that I'm far better at the people part of the business than the bookkeeping. As he began to look at how I had been running the business, he started asking about certain invoices and I snapped, "I don't know, Scott, I'm just cooking eggs and helping the customers."

Nyla's in Noblesville (1999-2004)

His voice intensified, "But you've gotta stay on top of invoices and make sure your taxes are paid, Nyla!"

I guess he had a point, but I was completely overwhelmed keeping up with demand and had no idea how to do the bookkeeping. He was the one who knew how to run a restaurant.

He gathered up whatever traces of receipts and paperwork he could find stacked in the office or stuffed into drawers, put them into a shoebox, and took them to a great friend of ours, Doug Cook, who is an attorney and accountant. Scott handed him the box and told him I hadn't kept track of anything and to help us know what to do from there.

Needless to say, the taxes that had accrued set us back once again. We lost some of the progress we had made toward the original debt because we now had to add tens of thousands more to our negative net worth.

You would think we would give up at that point and just file for bankruptcy. But we didn't want to close our doors or penalize the people we did business with for our mistakes. We were committed to being people of our word. It was tough, though. I understand why people give up. All we could do was keep going and keep learning. We would continue running Nyla's for five years while Scott worked at Applebee's and we kept chipping away at the debt.

I'll never forget the day I took the last of those tax checks to the courthouse downtown. After delivering it and having that tax bill paid in full, I sat on the curb outside the courthouse and wept.

CHAPTER FIFTEEN

THE BIG MIRACLE

Scott

In 2004, I was still a franchise consultant for Applebee's when our five-year lease was up at Nyla's. We needed to put money into that building to install a hood system for the kitchen, and the landlord was going to raise our rent, but we were still chipping away at that $300,000 debt that we'd been whittling down since 1992.

That's about when I discovered a restaurant on Morse Reservoir in north Noblesville that was for sale. A successful businessman in the area named Allen Rosenberg owned quite a bit of property that he and his son developed around the reservoir. The building he was renting needed a lot of work. When he took me through the building, I could envision exactly what I would do with it. I knew I could turn it into a profitable restaurant and bar that would draw people from the nearby housing developments and beyond, but it needed a lot of renovations.

I told the owner, "I love this property. I want to rent it, but I need some time to figure this out because we are paying off debt, and I don't know how I will finance it yet."

Nyla and I prayed about it and decided that if this was the right move for us, we would be given favor with the right people who could help us make it happen. We knew that banks don't often take risks on restaurants and that our debt would only create an additional hurdle to getting funding. I knew how to run a profitable restaurant. I just needed to figure out a way to fund it.

He agreed to give us some time, but in the meantime, he went to people I'd worked for in the past to get some background on me. He learned about my track record for building and managing successful restaurants. Meanwhile, he was visiting Nyla's, observing how Nyla operated, and observing the loyal customer base we had built there. He could see that we knew how to run a restaurant at this point.

Before long, I scheduled another meeting with him to walk through his building together. The landlord asked me, "What is your vision for this place?"

I told him exactly what I was seeing. I could envision exactly where I would situate the bar, how I would set it up, and what I would do to update the space. He asked how much funding I thought would be needed to get a restaurant up and running. I listed off the renovations that needed to be made, and he agreed. Then he added that he also felt that the parking lot would need an upgrade and better lighting. I agreed. We did a rough calculation of what the changes would cost, and it came to approximately $150,000

What happened next, I still can't believe. Allen looked at me and said, "Would you do this if I loaned it to you?"

I couldn't believe my ears. Was this man I had just recently met seriously going to be our bank so we could rent his property to open our own restaurant on Morse Reservoir?! It seemed too good to be true. Turns out, he was serious.

We drew up the agreement, closed Nyla's in Noblesville, and I set into the work of opening our first Wolfie's restaurant on Morse Reservoir. I needed to retain my salary and benefits from Applebee's while we built Wolfie's, so I would oversee the renovations, and obtain all the licenses, certifications, and inspections we needed to open while still maintaining my position with Applebee's.

Nyla would train the staff and manage daily operations at the restaurant once we opened, and I would help her create systems, manage the books, and oversee operations on the weekends when I wasn't traveling. The first three years of running Wolfie's were intense. Nyla worked probably eighty hours a week making sure everything was going well during the week without ever taking a salary so we could pay the staff, make our rent payments, and continue paying on the debt.

I would come in on the weekends and tell her what we needed to do better. This did not go over well at times, but I knew how to run a successful restaurant. We would often argue, sometimes pretty loudly, but it wasn't personal. We both wanted what was best for the business, we just didn't always agree on *how* to go about things. It was working!

Both of us brought something unique to the process. Nyla was always aware of how each employee was doing, she knew their stories and their life situations. She knew how to build a sense

of camaraderie among the staff and a feeling of
community among patrons. I excelled behind the
scenes, making sure the kitchen ran smoothly,
managing overhead and pricing, and making sure
we could make a profit while also giving people
the highest quality experience possible. If I felt like
a staff member wasn't pulling their weight, Nyla
would often advocate for them. You could say we
are the definition of "yin and yang" — opposites
in so many ways, yet stronger together because of
the way our differences compensate for each
other's weaknesses.

The growing success of Wolfie's was a dream
come true. We had been given a once-in-lifetime
opportunity to build a restaurant with our name
on it in this growing community, and people loved
it. When this man made it possible, we knew we
had been given a gift that had the potential to
change our lives forever. And it did. We were
never late on payments and threw ourselves into
making the restaurant a success, and paid him
back in full out of the proceeds.

Years later, that man stood next to me in front of his entire family and said, "One of the best investments I ever made was in this guy right here."

His words brought tears to my eyes. This guy had built an incredibly successful empire during his lifetime. He took a risk on me when no one else would, even though he barely knew me. Hearing those words from him was one of the most gratifying compliments of my career. I still get emotional when I think about it.

CHAPTER SIXTEEN

ENOUGH

Nyla

Ever since AAA went out of business in 1992 and Scott went back into restaurant jobs, I'd been fully invested in helping run our businesses. I loved working with people and creating places where members of our community loved to gather. It was a lot of work, but whether I was hauling mulch, problem solving, or training dining staff, it was always about the people for me.

While it was tough to give up what we had
built at Nyla's, we knew we couldn't pass up the
opportunity we had been given to open Wolfie's
on Morse Lake. We will always be grateful to that
local business owner for taking a chance on us,
and we were never going to make him regret his
decision to invest in us. Our first Wolfie's opened
on May 31, 2004, which was Scott's birthday.

Before long, the restaurant began attracting big
crowds and doing well, but it took every waking
hour of every day to build it and keep it going.
When we started Wolfie's both of the kids were in
high school, and during the next couple of years, I
was running the restaurant all day every day
during the week while Scott kept his full-time job
with Applebee's. Then Scott would come in on
Friday evening after traveling for work all week
and tell me everything I was doing wrong. I'll
admit, he was usually right about how we could
make things run smoother or tighten up our
procedures, but after spending all of my energy
trying to take care of everything in his absence, I

would get mad at him for critiquing decisions I had made. I'm sure the constant exhaustion didn't help my patience level either.

We have never held anything in when trying to work out our differences. I'm sure there were times when our staff wondered if we were going to recover, the way we argue openly. But we have to solve things at the moment. The restaurant business moves fast, and we can't put off conversations or let issues build steam; we don't have time for that. But we always come to some sort of agreement eventually, then tell each other, "Love you!" and move on. Nothing is left unsaid between us, so there isn't any room for resentment to grow. We know a lot of couples who have tried to work together and just couldn't do it, and that is understandable. We've had to learn how to communicate and not let anything fester that could potentially come between us

Ansley graduated and went to Bloomington for a couple of years. She and Alec were both good kids, but when she was gone, Scott was traveling

all the time, and I was running the restaurant all
hours of the day, Alec was alone, unsupervised, a
lot of the time. Parenting on my own all week
while trying to run Wolfie's was becoming
increasingly overwhelming. But then Scott would
get home and step in to help out, and we would
make it through another weekend.

It's always something at a restaurant. We were
constantly distracted, always troubleshooting or
figuring out how to solve problems. Not
surprisingly, we started having problems crop up
with Alec. He was spending more time with his
friends than he did with us, and soon we started
getting calls from his school that he was getting
into trouble. Ever since he was a little kid, the four
of us had always been like a little wolf pack, and
he had always been enthusiastic about helping
with the family businesses, but we could tell he
was drifting from us.

I knew all the signs and tricks kids might try
when they're trying to get by with things because
I'd done most of them myself when I was in high

school. But with everything going on, I couldn't keep an eye on him all the time. It was hard to see him pulling away and making decisions we knew weren't good for him. We would challenge him and try to get him to be honest with us about the decisions he was making, but our conflicts at home started becoming more and more intense. I was constantly on edge, worrying about what he was up to.

For three years, Scott had been traveling for Applebee's Monday through Friday when suddenly everything came to a head. One night, while he was in New York City trying to help an Applebee's franchisee recover during the aftermath of 9-11, I got a call that would stop me in my tracks.

I had come home late that night and fallen into bed, exhausted from another long day at the restaurant. But not long after I fell asleep, I was startled awake by a phone call. There's nothing that will jar you awake faster than a middle-of-the-night phone call when your kids and husband aren't home.

"Mom, I've messed up…"

It was Alec. He proceeded to explain that he took a girl home from a gathering with friends, and she'd accidentally left the purse in his car. On his way home from her house, he got pulled over for running a red light on 116th Street, and the officer began asking questions. The officer proceeded to search Alec's car and discovered marijuana in his friend's purse. Alec was arrested for possession of an illegal substance, his car was impounded, and he was calling from the Hamilton County jail.

I threw on some clothes and drove to the police station to pick Alec up. I posted bail, filled out the paperwork, and by the time I drove Alec back home it was almost time for me to be back at the restaurant. So, with almost no sleep, I dressed for work and drove to Wolfie's by 8:00 a.m.

That day was terrible. I was exhausted, and we were getting pounded at the restaurant.

Customers were coming at me; Alec was at home but I couldn't get to him; and I was so distraught that I started breaking out into hives.

That day was a breaking point for me. I was done. After twenty years of marriage and after spending most of those years working as hard as possible to pay back our massive debt load and gain some level of financial security, I had reached my limit.

I never interrupted Scott with phone calls when he was traveling. He was in an important meeting, but he picked up right away.

When he answered, I was bawling. I blurted out, "I'm done. I need you to come home. Alec is in trouble again, and I can't do this alone anymore."

Scott paused thoughtfully, then he said the one thing I needed most to hear at that moment…

"Okay, honey."

CHAPTER SEVENTEEN

ANOTHER MIRACLE

Scott

I was sitting in a nice restaurant in downtown New York City, meeting with my boss, the franchisee of the New York City Applebee's, two friends, and George Steinbrenner, owner of the New York Yankees, when my phone rang. When Nyla's name came up on my phone, I knew something was wrong. She never called me when I was in a meeting. I showed the phone to the franchisee, who was sitting next to me.

"This is not good," I told him.

"Yep. You'd better answer that," my colleague said under his breath.

"Hey, guys, excuse me, I've got to take this call," I said to the table of people.

I stepped away to answer Nyla's call and the second I answered I heard the desperation in her voice. She was crying and immediately began to tell me what was going on with Alec and how exhausted she was, not only because of the sleepless night she'd just had but because of the previous three years of long, stressful days managing Wolfie's in my absence. Her exhaustion and my absence during the week only compounded her worry and frustration over Alec because he was alone and unsupervised so much of the time after Ansley moved out. For someone with Nyla's capacity to rise to the occasion and do whatever she needed to do, this call meant she had reached her breaking point. She was crashing, and I knew if she was calling to ask me to come home, she was not okay. I assured her that I would be home as soon as possible.

When I stepped back to the conference table, my colleague said, "Everything okay?"

"Not really," I replied.

My boss spoke up: "Are you done?"

"Yep."

And just like that, I resigned from Applebee's, with George Steinbrenner still sitting across the table from me.

I knew it was time for me to stop traveling so I could be there for my family and run Wolfie's full time. Nyla had done her absolute best to manage the restaurant each weekday for three years without ever taking a salary. I knew she couldn't keep going like that without support. But we weren't sure how we could make it financially without that $100,000 in income.

When I got home, I had a serious father-son talk with Alec, as you might expect. He felt terrible about what happened. Even though the pot didn't belong to him, he knew he had been taking chances that weren't smart. He knew the path he was on could result in long-term consequences that he would have to live with for a long, long time.

I told him I would be quitting Applebee's after this, which got his attention. He knew I wouldn't have made that decision if I wasn't serious about showing up for my family when they needed me. They were more important to me than my job or income level. During the months that followed, we began to see him make better decisions for himself and his future.

I'm a family man first, but the businessman in me had to make this decision work financially. Nyla and I came up with a plan. I took a couple of months to fully transition from my role with Applebee's to help find my replacement, then set into making Wolfie's a full-time endeavor.

Alec learned some hard lessons that year, and I guess I have him to thank for giving me the push I needed to stop traveling and fully commit to our family and Wolfie's because we have never looked back since. That decision turned out to be the turning point, both for our family and for the success of Wolfie's. I knew it was the right move, even if I didn't know exactly *how* everything was going to happen.

I made some adjustments to the business, including a point-of-sale system that streamlined our processes, so we could run Wolfie's more efficiently. We also began creating fun event nights that brought people out to the restaurant on otherwise lower nights for business. We started hosting a trivia night, cornhole competitions, and special celebrations.

For years, our staff has joked, "If it weren't for Alec's pot-smoking days, Scott would still be working for Applebee's!" And though we can laugh about it now, it was a scary decision to give up the security of my full-time career. But Wolfie's began to thrive, and once again, Nyla, Ansley, Alec, and I worked together to make it happen.

About a year after quitting Applebee's, I drove Nyla over to a building in Fishers that I thought would make the perfect place for a second Wolfie's location.

"Wouldn't this little building make the coolest pub?" I asked Nyla.

"Shut up. We are not taking on anything else. I'm too tired," she blurted out.

I saw so much potential in it though. A few days later, Nyla went to visit her sister, so I decided to track down the owner, Joe Peterson, and set up a meeting while she was away. The building had previously been a Schlotzky's Deli and it was located off a busy exit from I-69, about twenty minutes away from Wolfie's at Morse Lake. The landlord didn't know me from Adam, but I called him up and expressed interest.

By the time we met at the building, Joe had already done some research on me. As usual, when we walked through the property I could envision exactly what I wanted to do with it. His building needed a lot of renovations, but I shared with him the potential I saw in it and he could see that I was serious about turning the space into another Wolfie's location.

We determined it would take around $300,000 to get the restaurant up and running. I told him I knew I could build a profitable restaurant there, but I needed to figure out how to find funding. Right then and there, he told me he would loan me the entire amount himself.

I could not believe my ears. This kind of thing never happens in the restaurant industry. But it happened twice for us.

"Let's do this," I said to Joe, beaming from ear to ear.

I knew I could not pass up this opportunity, so we shook hands on the spot. Then, I realized I was going to have to tell Nyla I had just bought a new restaurant. She thought I was crazy because she knew how much work it was to keep *one* restaurant going. Of course, she was right. But another thriving business would mean we could provide even more job opportunities in the area and help more people in our community.

Two men had taken a chance on me. Their belief in me changed my life. I have them to thank for opening the doors that would allow Nyla and me to create a new legacy in every way for our family. They also inspired me to be the kind of person who invested in people and created businesses that could make a difference in the lives of people and our community.

The building that would become the second
Wolfies, located in Fishers, Indiana.

CHAPTER EIGHTEEN

GROWTH

Nyla

I hate meetings. But I love parties. Everyone who works with us knows this. Since year one of Wolfie's, I have made sure we held annual retreats for managers and special seasonal gatherings for the staff. Scott and I believe in hard work, no doubt about it, but we also believe our people need to have fun together and celebrate outside of the restaurant.

When Scott and I worked at Dalt's so many years ago, our job was fun because our coworkers enjoyed each other's company. Several of those friends are still in our life today and some of them are working for us. Jeffrey, the bartender at Dalt's who let Scott live in his apartment years ago, has been a bartender at Wolfie's for years.

This is Jeffrey (center), the bartender at Wolfies at Geist, who offered Scott a place to live so many years ago.

Some staff members have been with us since the beginning and others for more than ten years, which is so rare in our industry. A few have left for other ventures, and some even returned to us a few years later. This is the kind of culture we have intentionally created.

The first management event we ever had included six people around our dining room table, which included managers and their spouses. The team has grown to nearly forty managers since that time, and there are hundreds of employees under them now. It has become harder and harder to know every person who works for any of our restaurants, but it's important to me to keep trying to find ways to connect with everyone who works for us.

After opening Wolfie's at Morse in 2004, Ansley started working for us when she came back from Bloomington. The moment she turned twenty-one she became the bartender, and we later promoted her to assistant manager with me. I trained her as manager for Wolfie's so she could eventually replace me.

After training to be a line cook at Nyla's as a kid, Alec started in the kitchen at Wolfie's and later became a server. When he turned twenty-one, we started training him for management, and in 2008, Alec became a manager at our second restaurant in Fishers.

The Fishers location opened in 2008, the same year the housing market tanked, which created a challenging economy for growing a restaurant, so we started having special parties and events during the week like trivia night, euchre night, and cornhole contests at both restaurants to bring people out for some lighthearted fun. We had bands come on special nights like the evening before Thanksgiving and New Year's Eve. Each Christmas, we continue a thirty-year tradition of having Santa visit, which we now call Lunch with Santa. These events have become traditions in the community that people look forward to, and it is such an honor to be part of their annual traditions.

A young pastor in the area started holding outreach events called Pub Theology, where a band played, then he gave a brief inspirational talk. Some of our regulars at the bar balked at having to sit through any mentions of God or faith, but our faith is an important aspect of our lives. Anytime someone complained about having to sit through a worship song or a prayer, I would tease them and ask how life without any sort of connection to God was working for them. We often got into good conversations because they knew we cared about how they were doing.

As a result of these events, we have seen people engage in conversations they never might have had otherwise. Some have even shown up at church after something they heard resonated with them. We have since added Worship on the Water, where we have a worship band come and play once a month, and it consistently brings some of the busiest weeknight crowds we get.

We are not religious fanatics by any stretch of the imagination. We just know how important it has been for us to have a spiritual foundation for our lives and businesses. Scott and I are far from perfect, but every good decision or opportunity that brought us to where we are now began with prayer. We are not shy about our belief in a God of second chances, and we know the spiritual principles that have guided us for the past forty years have not only been good for us but have helped us forge relationships of trust, integrity, and credibility in the community.

After the first two Wolfie's restaurants became profitable, Scott got a call from a friend about a space that used to be a pub called the Yorkshire Rose in Carmel, Indiana. When the Yorkshire Rose closed, Scott took his friend's recommendation and walked through it. The rest is history. He knew he could make it into another Wolfie's and that the location would work.

This time, we had two successful restaurants going for us, and we had finally paid off those old debts. So, Scott went to a bank in town to ask if they would be willing to give us a business loan to

Wolfie's in Carmel, Indiana

turn the old Yorkshire Rose into a third Wolfie's location.

For the first time in that bank's history, they took a chance on our restaurant and we opened a Wolfie's in Carmel in 2012. Since 80% of restaurants fail within the first five years of opening, this was unheard of at the time. As we have always done, we made on-time payments and established a strong relationship with our lender, and we continue to do business at this bank still today. This bank has since taken a chance on several other local restaurants, and those investments have been a win-win for them, the business owners, and the community.

Attached to the Carmel Wolfie's was a nail salon that ended up moving out of the space. We took over the additional space and turned it into an intimate bar setting called The Broken Barrel for twenty-one-and-up guests, which shared a kitchen with Wolfie's. Having both locations side-by-side enabled us to cater to family dining and provide exceptional food for the bar out of the same building.

In 2015, we opened a Wolfie's in Westfield, Indiana, which Alec opened pretty much by himself after Scott was done renovating it. Alec needed to take that one over because Scott was working on another place not far from there that we had been dreaming about for a while.

We love Italian food and wine, but we don't know how to cook authentic Italian food. So, we started looking for the right people to help us create a restaurant with that kind of specialty. Scott found a quaint little house in Westfield, Indiana, and gutted it to create a vibrant little place called The Italian House, which opened in Westfield just three months after we opened Wolfie's in Carmel. We decided to make The Italian House a dinner-only place, so it is only open from 5:00 p.m. to 9:30 p.m., which is easier to operate and staff due to the shorter shifts.

In 2018, we finally became completely debt-free. It was a monumental milestone, personally and professionally. That same year, a building at the marina of Geist Reservoir became available. This property was owned by the same landlord as our first Wolfie's, and he had been paid back in full since helping us open the Morse Reservoir property. We opened Wolfie's in Geist which, like our Morse Lake location, is nestled into a series of subdivisions on a reservoir, making it accessible by boat or by car, which caters uniquely to that

Wolfies at Geist Reservoir

community and has become another profitable investment.

In 2020, we opened Wolfie's in West Lafayette with the vision of it becoming a nice place for parents and college students to share a great meal not far from the Purdue University campus. You'll learn in the next chapter how that year impacted not only this new addition but all of our restaurants. But it is a great location that we knew had a lot of potential near the busy university.

Next to The Italian House, in Westfield, there was a funky building that looked like a barn. The owner had first shown it to Scott when we were looking for a location for the Italian house, but it wasn't conducive to what we wanted to do there. A couple of years later, we decided to reconsider the barn-like space for another kind of restaurant that was unlike any of the others.

We decided to rent it, and as usual, Scott did all the renovations himself so we could do it cost-effectively while also making sure the work was done well. Soon after we began the renovations, we discovered that it was on a floodplain. Getting the proper permits to do what we wanted to do with the property required a lot of extra time and effort. So, while we waited for all of the paperwork and approvals, we used the building to run an event and catering service so we weren't wasting the space.

Then, in 2023, twenty-five years after the first Nyla's closed, we brought it back better than ever. It is now a funky, twenty-one-and-older bar and restaurant that contains elements and artifacts from the original Nyla's in Noblesville. The one big difference is that I'm staying out of the kitchen this time. We created the menu and let our chef put the final touches on it. We keep the menu pared down to just ten entrees that we call "chef-inspired Americana" cuisine.

The Wolfie's in Pendleton, Indiana, is the first place we've ever built from the ground up rather than renovating an existing building. A building existed on the property, but it was not salvageable. For that reason, building this restaurant came with challenges we had never faced before, including the inflated price of building materials at the time we began building it. However, Wolfie's in Pendleton finally opened in late 2023 and became what Scott promised would be the last Wolfie's location we would open. I laugh when I say that because I'm not sure I believe him!

Across the street from Nyla's and The Italian House, we are building Swanky Mule, which only serves drinks and charcuterie. The idea is to create place for customers to enjoy drinks and snacks while waiting for a table at our other restaurants and it's due to open later in 2024. We continue to make improvements at each of our locations to draw in the community by offering an inviting setting, great atmosphere, fabulous drinks, and mouthwatering cuisine. We love creating places where people can't wait to come back.

Initially, Scott and I came up with all the ideas for menus, the chefs would prepare them with their flare and expertise and bring their ideas for specials, then we would make final decisions as a family. However, with the addition of the new locations, Alec started helping create the menus and continues to assist with creating menus. We have been hands-on in most areas of the restaurants, but the busier we've become with the addition of new locations the more we've had to trust our team to help us carry the load.

As we have grown, I've had to work harder at getting to know the employees better because our team has grown to more than 300 employees across all our locations. I used to know what was going on in every single one of our employees' lives, so staying in touch has become a bigger challenge. I love the people we depend on and want them to feel known and cared for. For that reason, keeping a good team dynamic remains important to us. To me, keeping the back house staff and the front of the house functioning as one team is always the goal.

Our family is big on second chances. We always say we don't fire people...they fire themselves. We are clear about our standards, and if people can't meet those expectations, they know they can't expect to stay. For that reason, we maintain a high retention rate.

We don't look for perfect people to work for us, and we certainly aren't perfect ourselves, but we hire people who have great personalities, who are willing to grow with us, and who work hard not only for the business but for the kind of legacy we want to create in this community.

CHAPTER NINETEEN
2020

Scott

Before 2020, we had survived the housing market crash of 2008, and the 2001 terrorist attacks on the World Trade Center in New York, which I spent years helping Applebee's navigate during the aftermath. Both of those scenarios were incredibly difficult, but nothing would compare to the challenges we would face in 2020.

In March 2020, when we opened Wolfie's in
West Lafayette, one mile from the campus of
Purdue University, we had no idea that the World
Health Organization was about to declare the
COVID-19 virus a public health emergency that
same month. We certainly couldn't have imagined
that more than 30,000 students would be required
to shelter in place and eventually vacate the
campus.

At this point, we had seven restaurant
locations across Central Indiana and we had to
reduce each restaurant's capacity from 100% to
25%, then to 0% at one point. With decreased
seating capacity, to allow people to be safely
spaced out across the restaurant, we had to move
to an entirely different business model and focus
on carryout orders as a major part of each
restaurant's bottom line.

Every location needed new carryout parking
signs and entirely different processes to
accommodate carryout orders. We needed an
entirely different menu with food that could be

transported more easily, as well as better containers and bags for the increased carryout business. Each new menu for each location would then need a QR code with online ordering capabilities so people could view the menu and order with their phones.

Before March 2020, our businesses did less than 2% in carryout orders, but when we were required to adhere to a 0% capacity during the height of the pandemic, we quickly had to turn into a 100% carryout restaurant across all our locations. All of the changes we made had to be implemented immediately, with almost no warning, along with even more stringent cleaning and sanitation measures than we already practiced.

The restaurant business is stressful on normal days. There are always variables when you are in the food service industry, and we have tried to navigate them with as much humor and grace as possible. But this year was, by far, more difficult than anything we have ever experienced, before or since that time. Every morning when we woke up, we had more questions than answers. Each day brought more to do than we could reasonably accomplish in one day.

We were determined not to lay off any of our full-time staff members, knowing they depended on this job for their survival. But the restaurants were operating at such decreased capacity that we started asking the staff to lean into their other skills — in most cases, skills that we had never needed from them before. Whether they were good at technology, painting, cleaning, or other tasks beyond what they typically did, we found ways to keep everyone busy so they could stay employed full-time.

Most of the restaurants in town were furloughing their workers, which created a ripple effect on families that impacted the entire community and beyond. Everything about working in the restaurant industry became harder, and because the protocols were changing every week, survival as a business became a moving target. The immense amount of time, creativity, and money it took to comply with all the requirements to stay in business caused intense strain on everyone.

Parents with young children were trying to manage their kids' education at home without any extra support. Most needed to work during the day, yet their kids were at home suddenly learning virtually from laptops instead of sitting in a classroom. All of this came with the reality that people all around us were getting sick, losing family members to the virus, and living in fear of getting sick.

For years, Nyla had been asking me to consider closing on Sundays to give our employees and ourselves one day to rest during the week. But when the pandemic hit, she became increasingly worried about the strain on everyone's families. We kept hearing of more restaurants all over town furloughing their workers and we were doing everything possible to avoid having to do that, so thinking of closing for even one day each week felt impossible.

Sunday was one of our busiest days. I'm a numbers guy, so for years I'd been telling Nyla, "Honey, you're talking about a two-million-dollars-per-year decision. That is how much we are going to lose in sales if we close on Sundays." We threw around the idea of closing on Mondays instead of Sundays since it's not such a busy day. But Nyla was insistent because taking Mondays off would not allow our employees to spend time with their families. On Mondays, kids would be in school and spouses would likely have to work. The point was to give families time to together to rest.

For the first few months of the pandemic, whenever Nyla and I decided to go to church before heading in to work, we noticed how tired and worn down everyone seemed. We could see how weary people were from trying to keep their heads above water. At our restaurants and everywhere else we turned, people were stressed and stretched thin.

Often, when services were over, we would have a barrage of texts waiting for us on the walk out to the car about emergencies happening at the restaurant that needed immediate attention. We would then spend Sunday afternoon trying to help the staff hold it all together.

We decided to pray about the idea of closing on Sundays. We asked for wisdom to make the best decision for everyone. And, if you remember what happened when Nyla prayed for a *little house on the prairie* years earlier, you can probably see where this is going.

I couldn't just give up two million dollars per year. But then I had to ask myself, "Who am I trusting?" Pretty soon, I knew what we had to do. We decided to invest back into our people by closing all of our restaurants on Sundays.

I could tell you all the reasons that was a crazy decision, but I can also tell you that when I chose not to lean on my own understanding, something miraculous happened. All I know is that we never had to lay off any of our full-time staff and all of the restaurants survived the pandemic. Later, I would see the numbers 4% percent after moving from a seven-day work week to six days.

It has always been important to us to treat people right, train them well, and support their overall well-being. But we especially noticed how this value paid off after deciding to give our people Sundays off. We were amazed at how much better the rest of the week went. Our turnover rates grew lower than most of the restaurants in our area because people love having Sundays off and it is so rare to find a restaurant that will take that kind of risk.

We don't have much turnover, and we don't have staffing issues, which is rare for any restaurant. I have friends and fellow business owners who stay open on Sundays and there are plenty of pubs people can go to, so we are happy to send our customers to those businesses on Sundays. But we have seen too many improvements in the staff's morale and attrition rates to ever question that decision.

During the COVID-19 shutdowns, Alec and Nyla started a podcast called "Nyla's Happy Half Hour" on YouTube to give people a reason to smile. They told stories people hadn't heard before about how we built Wolfpack Restaurant Group as a family.

No doubt about it, 2020 was a pivotal year. We were grateful to be operating debt-free by that point and to have had money in the bank. Otherwise, there would have been no way we could have helped all our staff remain employed and keep all our locations open.

The new restaurant at Purdue is now called Boomerang's, and along with all of our properties, is once again thriving. That is nothing short of a miracle that wouldn't have been possible without a lot of sacrifices and a hard-working team of people bringing together all of their skills to help us keep going.

So many restaurants had to close their doors forever during and after the COVID-19 pandemic. I can only credit the Lord for that nudge of consciousness telling me to trust, reminding me that doing right by our people was worth doing, no matter what it cost.

CHAPTER TWENTY
OUR LEGACY

Nyla

When Scott and I met, I wanted to be a professional tennis player. He always dreamed of being a professional football player. Now, forty years later, we are grateful those dreams never became a reality because we would have missed out on all the wild twists and turns that showed us what we were capable of. If things had gone according to our plans, we might never have created the legacy that will now carry on after we are gone.

I think back to how lonely I was in that first apartment when Scott was working long days and I was home with Ansley. That time in our life was a stark contrast to the parties and fun we had when we first met. But I learned things through that experience I couldn't have learned any other way.

I learned during those lonely, depressing hours years how to be with myself and accept reality while also continuing to dream and pray for the change I want to see in my life. I dug deep and found a level of authenticity with God that has sustained me through all of the ups and downs. I still rely on that faith every day.

I am more convinced than ever that faith is about acceptance and inclusion, never about judgment. Scott and I believe that loving people is the best possible way to express love for God. After all, love is what stays with us when everything else fades.

I'm not aware of any other husband-and-wife team that has built a community of restaurants without investors or partners and without losing their marriage or kids. We have a lot to be grateful for. I know our wisdom, alone, never would have been enough to guide us through this wild ride we've been on together for the past forty years.

Both of our kids have families of their own now, and they are helping to manage the restaurants. Somewhere along the way, they became our dearest friends in the world, and we are grateful for the way they have brought their strengths, intellect, and creativity to what we do.

Maybe because I loved living near my grandmother and aunt as a kid, one of the dreams I always hoped and prayed for was to own enough land for our entire family to be able to live near one another on the same piece of property. When we first moved into the home Scott renovated in rural Noblesville, we were grateful to own a beautiful white house on five acres with trees surrounding the property. It was even better than the rental house at Conner Prairie, and it was all ours. We eventually hoped to build a second house for my parents on that same piece of land, but the city would only permit one home per five acres in our location. So, Scott built additions to the white house, starting with a gorgeous, spacious family room, then he added a large attached garage with a beautiful in-law apartment above it for my parents. They loved it, and we didn't have to build a second house to give them a nice, comfortable place to retire.

In rural Noblesville, local landowners who are selling off land typically give their neighbors the first opportunity to buy it before putting acreage up on the market. After living in the white house for seventeen years, our neighbor allowed us to purchase a few more acres connected to our property, which came with a house and a barn.

Scott renovated the house on the additional property, then he and I moved into it. He then added an event barn within walking distance of the house, which has office space, a conference room, and a lodge-style meeting space with a gorgeous twenty-foot bar, a kitchen, a fireplace, and space for all kinds of gatherings and employee parties.

My parents loved their apartment and didn't want to go anywhere, so we asked Ansley if she and her family wanted to rent the white house. She agreed, and they still live there today.

The white house after Scott renovated and added
the family room and in-law quarters.

We loved our new house and barn, and I felt so blessed to be there; there was just one aspect of living there that started wearing on me. Every time I looked out of the kitchen window, I was staring at a junkyard on the neighboring property. There were old, dilapidated semi-trailers that had been sitting so long they were rusted and falling apart. Over time, they had become driven down into the ground by season after season of weathering. There were old tires and trash that had been thrown into a huge pit in the ground and it was a terrible eyesore.

I contacted the person who was leasing the land, who put us in touch with the owner. Then I negotiated an offer on this property that adjoined to ours, and the owner accepted our offer. But then we had to figure out what to do with all of the junk that had been left behind. The work ahead of us felt overwhelming at first, but like everything else we've ever done, we jumped in and did what we had to do.

We uncovered a small barn-like structure that had been overgrown with trees and brush. When we got inside of it, we were devastated by what we saw. The remnants left behind told a story of human trafficking that had happened

The dilapidated structure before renovation.

right under our noses before the property was abandoned. The vandalism and barbaric conditions inside that building sent cold chills up our spines, and we knew before we began any further renovations, we needed to pray over this place and clear out any darkness or bad energy lingering there. We walked through the house asking any darkness to leave and asking divine light to infiltrate this space. We invited God's wisdom, peace, and blessing into the entire property.

Inside the old semi-trailers were carnival prizes like stuffed animals and other trinkets, indicating that whoever had owned them must have once been part of a traveling carnival. Scott contracted a crew that removed ten dumpsters that each held forty cubic yards of trash from the lot, all of which were leftovers from people who were obviously involved in disturbing tragic human rights violations.

Scott got the small barn completely stripped down to the studs so it could be rebuilt entirely. We were grateful to be able to transform the property where so much pain had happened into a joyful, peaceful place. Seeing the pile of junk and dilapidated trailers become a beautiful addition to our property brings me pure happiness now whenever I look out the kitchen window.

Scott also renovated a small house that had also been left on the property, which we planned to rent out. When the renovation was done, it was beautiful. Alec asked what we were planning on doing with it and inquired about renting it from us. Soon, Alec and his wife and kids moved in. They now live just down the hill and through a small tree-lined clearing from our house.

My dad passed away in 2022. He and Mom lived in the apartment Scott built for them until that time. Mom still happily lives there and, at this moment, we feel so blessed to have four generations of family living on our property.

Because my grandma and aunt were such an important part of my best childhood memories, I always imagined how fun it would be for our kids and grandkids

My parents, Matthew Peelen (November 6, 1936 — August 29, 2022) and Sandy Peelen

to have those kinds of memories with Scott and me. Seeing that dream become a reality has been incredible, even though none of it came easily.

We have established one important boundary for ourselves: we always call each other before dropping by, so each family has a sense of our own space and privacy. Not long ago, however, our ten-year-old grandson broke the rule when showed up at our door crying. He was so upset and told us that his parents were mad at him and that he was running away from home. I assured him that we would get this worked out and took him back home on a golf cart, where he and his parents could talk it out. I love being there for those moments in my family's life. I thank God every day for what we have together.

We work a lot, but whenever we get together for family dinners or bonfires, we try to stay off our phones so we can be present. We love the work we do, but it's important to us that all our family memories aren't centered around the restaurants.

Alec and Ansley both learned things about running a business that college students never learn in a classroom. They have gotten real-life experience since those early days of selling produce and landscape supplies out of the pole barn at Hillsdale. They have lived and breathed restaurant management and leadership along with us since they were kids, and they continue to willingly participate in the family business. Years of on-the-job training have shaped them into great leaders in the company. Scott and I couldn't imagine running our businesses without them.

We are beyond grateful that our kids have grown into such great people who still want to work with us. And we are equally thankful that we could give our family the support and opportunities that we worked so hard to be able to provide.

We love what we have built in the suburbs of Indianapolis. We haven't just built businesses, we have built relationships, which to us, is what creating a legacy is all about.

Alec recently asked to meet with us because he had something important he wanted to talk about with us. During that meeting, he expressed his heartfelt concern that we are still working at the same intensity we have for more than thirty-five years. He told us he wanted us to be around for a long time and that he and Ansley wanted to help us enjoy what we have built at this stage of our lives. We had also been feeling a shift happening inside us, knowing we wanted to begin stepping back and letting our team do more and more of the daily operations at the restaurants. So this conversation happened at just the right time. We were ready to start enjoying what we had built.

The year 2024 marks our fortieth wedding anniversary, the the twentieth anniversary of Wolfpack Restaurant Group, and the publication of this book. We are ready to turn the page and move into a new phase of life where we can celebrate all that we have worked so hard to achieve.

Documenting this story is a key part of that shift. It is important to us that the people who enjoy our restaurants know all of the blood, sweat, and tears that have gone into creating gathering places where our community could gather for delicious food, well-crafted drinks, an inviting atmosphere, and extraordinary service. Scott personally poured his creativity, carpentry skills, and restaurant management abilities into creating every single location. Every table, booth, and doorknob is there because he put it there. And I have loved connecting with the people, training our service staff, and getting to know their stories.

The human resources department has always been *us*, and we value every single person who has helped us make our restaurants what they are. We have invested ourselves into each location to make it something special and have intentionally created environments where people want to be—the kind of family atmosphere that reflects our care for people and our commitment to excellence.

It hasn't been a walk in the park, but we've had a lot of fun.

The food, the service, the atmosphere, and the memories made around our tables all reflect part of who we are. This business was created *by* real people, *for* real people. To every employee, patron, community member, business owner, friend, or family member who reads these pages, we hope our story helps you understand what is possible for *you*, too.

We live in constant gratitude for those who believed in us, took chances on us, and helped make it all possible. We understand adversity, loneliness, and second chances and we hope this story serves as a reminder that no matter how grim things may seem, there is always a way forward. You are capable of more than you might realize.

To future generations of our family, it's important to us that you know where you have come from. You are part of a legacy of hard work, honesty, faith, and love. Oh, and fun! Lots of fun.

We speak our minds, but we do it out of care for one another. We fight *for* the things that are important to us, but never *against* anyone's well-being. No matter what paths you take in your life, we hope you always live out that legacy of acceptance and kindness, because this world needs a whole lot more of those things.

If you remember nothing else about this story, remember that failure never has to be the final chapter of your story. It might just be the beginning. The humility and lessons that come with making mistakes have the power to make us all wiser, more successful, and probably a lot more pleasant to be around. Failure is a much better teacher than getting everything right the first time.

Only a handful of people knew our story before now, so we hope these pages not only offer you a glimpse into the history of Wolfpack Restaurant Group but also encourage you to reflect on your legacy. We hope you will be inspired to let your greatest challenges propel you toward your best days yet.

Keep dreaming, praying, showing up to the work in front of you, and doing the next right thing. Over time, you begin to see what is possible, not only for you but also for those who come behind you. Who knows, you might find that doing right by people and following your instincts helps you leave the world a little better than you found it.

When you live in gratitude and remember the people who helped you along the way, you will more than likely realize that you have the opportunity to help someone else with what you've learned. There is nothing quite like getting to pay it forward and help others who come after you. That is a great moment.

Every wolf pack has an alpha couple. That has been us almost as long as we can remember. Now, as we begin a new chapter, we are excited for the chance to empower those who helped us get this far. Wolfpack Restaurant Group will continue our long tradition of excellence and care for everyone who walks through our doors. We are excited to see the restaurants we've built continue to be a light in our community. Now, twenty years after that first business owner took a chance on us so we could open Wolfie's in 2004, we understand why he did it. We finally see how it feels to invest in people you believe in and later come to realize they were the best investment we would ever make.

Our Wolfpack - November 2023

MEET THE AUTHORS

Scott & Nyla Wolf

Scott and Nyla Wolf are the dynamic duo behind Wolfpack Restaurant Group and owners of six Wolfie's Grill restaurants, as well as Broken Barrel, The Italian House, Nyla's, Boomerang's, and Swanky Mule (coming in 2024). Celebrating 40 years of marriage and the 20-year anniversary of their first Wolfie's restaurant with the 2024 release of Wolves In the Kitchen, their number one priority is leaving legacy for their family and community. For more about Wolfpack Restaurant Group and restaurant locations, visit wolfpackrestaurantgroup.com. For copies of Wolves In the Kitchen or media requests, visit wolvesinthekitchen.com.

Emily Sutherland

Emily Sutherland is a career storyteller who spent more than 20 years in the music industry, honing her craft behind the scenes as a ghostwriter, videographer, content creator, and scriptwriter for video and television. Since 2017, she has helped dozens of individuals write their stories and launch them into the world. A ghostwriter, collaborator, writing coach, course creator, and screenwriter, she draws from a wide range of storytelling experiences to help high profile speakers, trauma survivors, artists, business owners, and hometown heroes find their voice and tell their stories. Connect with her at emily@emilysutherland.me.